# Emerging Colombia

# Emerging Colombia

By JOHN M. HUNTER
*Department of Economics*
*Michigan State University*

Public Affairs Press, Washington, D. C.

For KT, Judy, Ginny, and Cindy, whose company is indispensable,
and for Alfonso, Eduardo, Gloria, Guillermo, Lelia, Pacha,
Patricia, and Tony who, among many others, made
two years in Colombia a privilege.

Copyright, 1962, by Public Affairs Press
419 New Jersey Avenue, S.E., Washington 3, D. C.

Printed in the United States of America
Library of Congress Catalog Card No. 62-18454

# ACKNOWLEDGEMENT

Considerable gratitude is due the Office of International Programs and the All University Research Fund, both of Michigan State University, for their assistance in support of this volume.

J.M.H.

226479

# Contents

# Prologue

"For my part, I travel not to go anywhere, but to go.  I travel for travel's sake.  The great affair is to move."
— ROBERT LOUIS STEVENSON, *Travels with a Donkey*

In the past twenty years more United States citizens have travelled and lived abroad than ever before, and it is inevitable that they have written about their experiences.  One result is a host of books concerning far-away places which generally fall into three categories.  The tourist book is designed to guide the traveler in a pleasant, comfortable journey.  The adventure book entertains, informs, and amazes.  Perhaps more numerous is the scholarly treatise, product of social scientists, singly and in teams, whose post-World War II assignments have taken them from continent to continent and back again; such treatises are not usually directed to the lay reader, but are to communicate new and exciting truths to colleagues or to report findings to a sponsoring agency.

This fits none of these categories well. It has a similar origin—the extraordinary and fortunate circumstances of living and working abroad for an extended period.  It is not a systematic and comprehensive study and reveals no great truths regarding Colombian society or its economic development.  However great the temptation to undertake some tourist promotion, this is not a travel book although the Hunters travelled widely and undoubtedly "know" Colombia much better than most Colombians.  Only in a special sense is it an "adventure" book, but there were adventures aplenty.  One does not soon forget a family trek by jeep and mule to an emerald mine.  Rather, it is a "professional adventure" book, as it recounts the impressions and activities related to my experiences as an economist from August, 1958 to August, 1960 in Colombia.

❊    ❊    ❊

As this is a frankly personal account, my background is relevant. "Itchy feet" must be an inherited characteristic.  As a youngster in a midwest professorial family in the 'twenties and 'thirties, the "travel bug" became fully developed.  Careful manipulation of the family budget permitted us to see most of the United States and eventually took us as far "abroad" as Quebec, Havana, and Tiajuana. More ambitious tourism was financially impossible. Travel in Europe was rare, and I remember wondering if we would ever see again a friend's family —Germany-bound on some sort of grant.

This is sharp contrast to the opportunities of the present university community. Thanks to the Agency for International Development (and its predecessors), the foundations, Senators Fulbright and Mundt, the world has literally opened up to the university scholar. The "stay-at-home" professor, while still a majority, no longer sees a colleague leaving for a foreign land with trepidation or as a unique case. On the contrary, the "floating" staff has become an academic problem. For some, these opportunities abroad provide personally satisfying work; they bring to the stateside classroom a great deal more life, reality, and knowledge when the itinerant professor returns.

This professor has wandered widely and well. As an infantryman redeployed from Europe, I was assigned in 1945 to an agency of the Department of State in Manila. This first exposed me to the problems and processes of economic development of the poorer countries, and the years 1947-50 were devoted to pursuing these interests in a couple of graduate schools. In 1955-56, now married with three daughters, I was a part of the Viet Nam Technical Assistance Group in Saigon as a faculty member of Michigan State University. After two years back on the campus I was appointed as director, Centro de Estudios sobre Desarrollo Económico[1] at the University of the Andes in Bogotá, Colombia. We arrived there late in August, 1958, and it was experience in this position which now induces the inevitable professorial activity of recording what one knows (or thinks he knows) for the benefit (he hopes) of posterity.

Many do not understand the Hunter family penchant for these kinds of experiences. We leave behind our friends, our house, and the contacts and "politicing" found in any human organization. The new environment is strange, we know no one, schooling for the kids may be a problem, hazards to health are greater, we may have a new language to learn. Why do we do it?

The only satisfactory way to gratify our basic curiosity about other people is to live among them. Opportunities for accomplishment and to be of service are enormous. Underdevelopd countries are the laboratories and text books of my special interests, and presumably I return a better teacher. Much more pragmatic are the following: It is thrilling and flattering to meet presidents and to count ministers among one's friends. There is a great sense of accomplishment to be able to communicate in a foreign language. Generally, too, the salary connected with these assignments is somewhat better than that in the States. With good luck and planning, in the past few years we have visited Japan, Hong Kong, Singapore, Angkor Wat, Quito, Lima, La Paz; we have had wonderful family vacations in Hawaii, Acapulco, and the Virgin Islands. Compare this to the opportunities available to the academic family of two decades ago!

Beyond these attractions, and perhaps most important of all, this is a wonderful education for our youngsters. This was forcibly impressed upon us in a rather strange way. In the course of reading to them one of the Bobbsey Twin series, we came across an account of a tribe of Romany speaking gypsies which, because of its strange tongue, was unceremoniously escorted out of the Bobbsey home-town. Subsequently, of course, the point was made that these gypsies *were* people and really quite nice ones even-if-they-did-speak-another language.

Some of the real effects of our living abroad were apparent when I had to stop to try to explain how and why prejudice against non-English speaking peoples had developed. At that time, the girls had lived roughly half their lives in an environment where English was not spoken, and they could not understand that speaking a foreign language was something somehow "strange". If nothing else were gained, having children grow up with such healthy attitudes would make overseas experiences worth-while.

❀     ❀     ❀

Three general works on the Colombian economy already exist,[2] and another would to a large extent be duplication. All three were the work of teams of experts with resources far beyond my own. Further, much of my time was spent in the daily tasks of administration, so that extended research into the problems and nature of the Colombian economy and society was not possible. On the other hand, I did some research and was involved in more. And I made it a point to learn what I could of the environment. The essays which follow, then, are opinions and impressions based upon two years of living and working in Colombia.

# Contrasts

"Contrariwise," continued Tweedledee, "if it was so, it might be; and if it were so, it would be: but as it isn't, it ain't. That's logic."
—LEWIS CARROLL

To describe Colombia in general terms one can only resort to the badly overworked "it's a land and society of great contrast" so frequently said of most underdeveloped countries. However accurate this may be in the general case of other nations, it has special applicability to Colombia. Only in the context of contrast can one approach an understanding of this lovely and neglected country.

*       *       *

The dominant feature of Colombian economics has been and always will be its geography. Superficially, the country is about the size of Texas and California combined (439,521 square miles in Colombia; 426,032 in the two named states). But the huge eastern plains (*llanos*) have almost no economic or political role in the present configuration of the country.

These plains extend almost the length of Colombia east of the mountains. In the north there are limitless, grassy flat lands, water-soaked much of the year, with meandering streams and major rivers wandering through the countryside. They appear from the air as the Great Plains of the midwest must have looked to the first white men. But they are low and nearly on the equator, so closer inspection reveals that the foliage bordering the streams is tropical jungle—the home of monkeys, parrots, and other game. As one goes south toward the sub-equatorial borders with Brazil, Ecuador, and Peru, grass lands become scarce and almost unexplored. A large party was completely lost for days in a minor penetration of the forests in 1960.

Colombian political organization recognizes the second-class status of the *llanos*. The major political divisions[1] of the country are *departamentos* (roughly corresponding to our states); areas of distinctly secondary importance are *intendéncias,* and the presently insignificant areas are *comisarías.* Of the seven geographical subdivisions of the plains, four are commisariats, two are intendancies, and from July,

1960, one (Meta) is a department. A glance at estimated data indicates the relative unimportance of the plain area and explains the lack of attention given it in accounts of Colombia.

| Political Division[a] | Square Miles | Persons per Square Mile |
|---|---|---|
| Arauca | 9,972 | 0.56 |
| Vichada | 39,764 | 0.14 |
| Meta | 32,903 | 0.91 |
| Vaupes | 58,867 | 0.07 |
| Caquetà | 41,052 | 0.60 |
| Putumayo | 10,225 | 1.36 |
| Amazonas | 48,007 | 0.07 |
| | 240,799 | |

The plains, then, are a huge chunk of land—slightly smaller than the state of Texas and with fewer people than North Dakota. In other terms, this 54.8 per cent of Colombia's land area includes only 16 per cent or so of the total population. These people and this area should not be ignored, but they are not an integral part of the economy, and one cannot afford to spend a disproportionate amount of time on them.

In order to eliminate the *llanos* from further consideration, a few comments are useful before returning to the remainder of the country. (1) I spent a week or more in the northern section travelling by jeep and by air. The furthest point reached was mid-Vichada where we visited a mission school. The use of Spanish at this outpost is far from general. Most of the Indians rely on pre-Columbian languages and can communicate between tribes only with the greatest difficulty. I bought here a pendant with various mystical qualities made from animal teeth. Conspicuously imbedded in the charm was a chip of ordinary bottle glass which speaks eloquently of the degree of "civilization" in this particular region. Weapons for war, hunting, and protection are crude bows and arrows, the latter made of reeds and tipped with wood or bone. Scarce metal is reserved only for those arrows destined to be fired at big game, notably the "tiger." Travel in this area is largely by foot and more commodiously by canoe. (2) This is real frontier country. Land is free for the taking (except close to the mountains) although it is supposed to be officially surveyed. Law and order is the responsibility of the land-owner, and he courts disaster by failing to provide adequate protection. Much of the land is held by absentee owners who frequently know neither how much land they own nor the number of cattle grazing on it. (3) Maps of the area are dotted with representations of airports, particularly in the north. These airports do exist but their "construction" consists only of chopping off the high grass, making certain that there are no great holes, and putting up two sticks to mark the end of the runways. The busy Bogotano cannot afford the hours of jeep or horseback riding required in the best of weather in order to visit his property.

Romance and beauty aside, why have the *llanos* remained dormant and what of their future? Topography is the most important consideration. Bogotá is at an altitude of 8,626 feet and Villavicencio, the gateway to the plains is at 1,633 feet. And one must climb another 1,500-2,000 feet just east of Bogotá to begin descent to the flat lands. Although less than fifty air miles separate the two cities, the road is more than twice this long and is something less than a good road. For months, it was open to daylight traffic only one hour daily while a landslide was cleared and repairs made. Transportation, especially of high-bulk commodities such as live cattle, is an expensive business and during rainy seasons an uncertain one.

Another central problem is intraregional transportation. A few roads exist, but penetration of the area by vehicle except in the dry season (said to be three months) is difficult and mostly impossible. These "roads" are, in most places, little more than worn tracks across the grass lands. I visited Trinidad, Boyacá°, in one of the more easily reached sections. Cattle produced here can be driven to market (Villavicencio) only during the dry season, and the 160 mile "drive" requires 25-30 days. During the wet season, this community is inaccessible except by river barge. During the dry season it can be reached by vehicle and is served by DC-3.

Hydrographic characteristics also contribute to the lack of development. The area drains into the Orinoco and Amazon Rivers which flow away from national markets, and the international markets to which they lead are severely limited. Exporting to Venezuela has greater potential than to interior Brazil, but Colombian policy has discouraged exportation of animals and animal products. These are the only current export possibilities of the plains.

There has been no systematic investigation of soil fertility. Enthusiasts report great potential and the ability to grow anything in prodigious amounts. On the other hand, others report the soil badly leached and essentially sterile. In any case, any massive movement of fertilizers into the area is now economically out of the question.

A discovery of major oil deposits would greatly improve the prospects of this area. It would require and perhaps finance the improvement of intra- and interregional transportation. As yet, exploration has not been encouraging. It is also rumored that a huge and rich deposit of bauxite exists in the Macarena region some 200 miles south of Villavicencio, but this is unconfirmed and no definitive exploration has been undertaken.

The plains will become increasingly important as expanding population puts more and more pressure on existing sources of foods, but it is doubtful that they are destined to become Colombia's breadbasket as some expect.

\* \* \*

The "real" Colombia is roughly the size of California with a population about that of New York state (13,000,000). This, too, is a land of great contrast and is dominated by its geography.

At the Ecuadorian border, the great Andes divide into three distinct ranges or *cordilleras*. One range proceeds up the west (Pacific) coast of the country. Between this and the central chain is the Valley of the Cauca River where Colombia is establishing a small scale T.V.A. The Rio Magdalena flows between the higher central range and the massive eastern mountain system. There is no adequate way to describe these ranges, but unless one can have some idea of their size, it is impossible to visualize the problems geography imposes on the country. Some notion of the terrain can be acquired by imaginary journeys from Bogotá to two of Colombia's other principal cities, Cali and Medellín. One must visualize these trips on U.S. highways of thirty or more years ago and remember that these roads constitute the life stream of the nation.

| Place | Miles from Bogotá | Altitude in Feet | Average Temperature |
|---|---|---|---|
| Bogotá | 0 | 8,626 | 55.4 |
| San Miguel | 22.9 | 8,987 | |
| Melgar | 65.2 | 1,410 | |
| Giradot | 82.6 | 1,069 | 82.4 |
| Ibagué | 131.7 | 4,100 | 71.6 |
| La Linea | 174.0 | 10,660 | |
| Calarcá | 188.3 | 5,310 | 66.2 |
| Cali | 334.3 | 3,289 | 77.0 |

As we leave the capital, we stay on the plateau for some twenty miles, even climbing a little to get to the rim of the *sabana de Bogotá*. At San

Miguel, we begin to descend almost constantly on a narrow winding highway to Melgar. Almost certainly after a heavy rain it will be necessary to wait until one or more landslides are cleared away. In that forty-two miles of road, the vertical change is 7,377 feet, nearly a mile and a half, or an average descent of 3.4 per cent. Another comparison indicates that this is about the same vertical distance as exists between Denver and the top of Pikes Peak. Jackets and sweaters are shed in a hurry as we pass from "cold" through "temperate" to "tropical country." As startling is the change from the austere vegetation and agriculture of the savanna to the riotous flora of more temperate climes to the tropical growth of the Magdalena River valley.

From hot Giradot on the river at 1,069 feet, we climb gradually to Ibagué and then more precipitously to La Linea at 10,660 feet in a little less than 100 miles. This is a climb of 3,000-4,000 feet less than ascending Pikes Peak from sea level. The maximum gradient on this road occurs between La Linea and Calarcá as we descend the central range, an altitude change of some 5,000 feet in fourteen miles or an average of about 7 per cent. No railroad yet crosses this range although several contruction attempts have been made.

The remainder of the trip to Cali, a major industrial and agricultural center, is pleasant and easy as we descend into the Valley of the Cauca and then travel through it. Fom Cali both a railroad and highway cross the western range to Buenaventura, the Pacific port where many of the imports destined for Bogotá arrive. An engineer friend reported receiving imported furnace brick in Bogotá from Buenaventura by truck at an average speed of nine miles per hour!

In less detail, we examine the profile of the direct route from Bogotá to Medellín, Colombia's "Manchester" and second city. It should be noted, however, that this is not the usual route because the road is poor and the gradients severe. Most vehicle traffic goes up the Cauca valley and crosses by the familiar route Calarcá-Ibagué.[4]

| Place | Miles from Bogotá | Altitude in Feet | Average Temperature |
|---|---|---|---|
| Bogotá | 0 | 8,626 | 55.4 |
| Alban | 36.6 | 7,366 | |
| Villeta | 59.9 | 2,761 | |
| Honda | 100.7 | 751 | 84.2 |
| Mariquita | 113.0 | 1,755 | 80.6 |
| Fresno | 129.2 | 4,887 | |
| Paramo de Letras | 165.9 | 12,083 | |
| Manizales | 189.5 | 7,061 | 62.6 |
| Medellín | 353.6 | 4,877 | 69.8 |

Again, we leave the savanna abruptly, this time just before reaching Alban. Here must be one of the world's most glorious views—coming off this huge table land to look down into a magnificent valley filled with mountains. We reach Honda on the Rio Magdalena and could take a side trip on down the river a few miles to La Dorada, the highest navigable point on the river. Honda is said to be the hottest city in Colombia. Goods arriving in La Dorada, or at ports lower on the river, can come by rail or by truck to Bogotá, having still a mile and a half of vertical distance to climb. The first sixty-five miles out of Honda is rough; we climb from almost sea level to over twelve thousand feet, an average grade of 3.3 per cent. Just to the south of this pass lies one of Colombia's several snow-capped peaks—17,000 foot Nevado del Ruiz. Manizales is the coffee capital of Colombia. This valuable export commodity must somehow find its way to the sea. Much of the coffee (329,238 metric tons exported in 1958) begins its journey by overhead cable car between Manizales and Mariquita—a road distance of seventy-seven miles. I had no occasion to investigate the economics of this operation, but superficially it appears to be a very sensible way of overcoming the difficulties of a *poor* road over terrain which offers no possibilities of a railroad. The rest of the journey to Medellín involves rugged country for the midwesterner, but it is not nearly so spectacular.

Bogotá until recently had no rail connections with either coast. The Ferrocarril del Atlántico, just completed, provides new service to the north coast ports of Barranquilla, Santa Marta, and Cartagena. This facility will reduce dependence on river traffic, more romantic, but less certain and avoid the long haul to Pacific coast ports. Domestically, it will integrate a vast land area into the metropolitan economy. Rail freight from the Pacific port of Buenaventura reaches Armenia on the western approaches to the central range. Here it is off-loaded and transhipped by truck over the mountains where once again it can continue its rail journey to Bogotá. Colombian railroads are not transplanted New York Centrals. One of the principal lines—Bogotá to Honda—for example, has a maximum capacity of eight loaded cars on its twisting, turning, narrow-gauge track.

Thus, Colombian geography provides for much of the contrast—from the tundra-like *paramos* to equatorial tropics; from the deserts of the upper Magdalena and the Guajira (a peninsula extending into the Caribbean) to the jungles of Choco bordering on Panama with nearly 300 inches of annual rainfall; from temperate climate products of potatoes, wheat, barley to tropical products of bananas, cotton, rice, orchids, papaya, etc.  Coffee, shade grown, has already been mentioned as the most important export commodity.  Abroad, Colombia is noted for its exotic emeralds, lovely gems found in the pre-Columbian mines at Muzo and Chivor and at Gachala—all within a day's travel of Bogotá. It is also a major producer of platinum and produces some gold, although neither contribute very much, in percentage terms, to total exports.

This overwhelming geography has many implications, and constant reference to the physical environment must be made because it *is* Colombia.  To re-emphasize its importance, there are two additional illustrations before passing on to other matters.  (1) In the course of our work, we became very familiar with the departament of Tolima.[5] Reference to a map indicates the central location of this department as well as its position across the principal highway Bogotá-Cali and the road to Neiva.  It has long been a politically and economically important departament.  Yet, even primitive roads do not reach all the *municipios,* and it is necessary for the governor (during this period a man of about sixty) to travel three days by horse or mule to reach the remotest of these.  One can imagine the difference between life in the seats of these *municipios* as compared to the lovely capital of the departament, Ibagué.  (2) In journeying around the country, one is never told "how far" it is to any place.  Rather, all distances are cited in time—"three hours to here or two hours to there."  And a wise informant looks carefully over the vehicle and its driver before making his pronouncement.  Vertical changes and road conditions are so important that there is little relation between road miles and time required. From my office in Bogotá on clear days I could see the snowcaps of the central range.  By air they are 100 miles away, but it takes nearly seven hours of driving to reach them.

Colombia's demographic development contrasts with that of most other Latin American countries.  The usual pattern is one major city about which economic activity is centered.  This is not the case in Colombia.  Rather, each region has developed its center, and each is independently important.  A functional map of Colombia would not resemble a wheel with all the spokes leading to Bogotá (as Venezuela is dominated by Caracas, for example) but a series of wheels with complex interrelations between them.  Prominent hubs in this sophisticated economic and political matrix are listed on the next page.[6]

| City | Population | Comments |
|------|-----------|----------|
| Bogotá | 1,064,740 | Capital, industry, agricultural trading, finance commerce |
| Cali | 503,530 | Industry, agriculture, transportation |
| Medellín | 545,860 | Industry, commerce |
| Barranquilla | 392,330 | Industry, shipping |
| Manizales | 156,270 | Coffee |

In all there are ten or more cities with populations of more than 100,000.

Colombia is an "underdeveloped and developing" economy as opposed to "underdeveloped and not developing." This characteristic accounts for additional contrast. Thus, its appearance, characteristics, and problems are vastly different from other economies which are poor and stagnant (*e.g.*, Viet Nam, Cambodia, Bolivia). Colombia is poor, but many segments of the economy are in motion, and the old exists alongside the new. Cases in point: rice harvested with $30,000 U.S. mechanical monsters and potato fields plowed by oxen; modern textile factories and others making textiles almost by hand; modern industrial societal complexes and Indians who still have no truck with the white man (the dangerous Montalones on the Venezuelan border); the hemisphere's oldest commercial airline (second oldest in the world) but tremendous bulk moved by burro and dugout, etc.

The present political arrangement is like none other that I know. Essentially, the two major parties have agreed to share on an equal basis and for sixteen years the political offices of the land. This development and its implications are the subject of the next chapter.

Toward the end of our stay, Colombia was experiencing a major appreciation of its currency. This made it rare in a world prone to depreciation. In December, 1958, we received pesos for dollars at a rate of 8.13 to 1 and before that seldom at less than 8. A complex of circumstances and policies led to a steady appreciation of the peso so that in May, 1960, the rate had steadily declined to about $6.80.[7] After a short time in Bogotá, we identified ourselves with the fortunes of Colombians; thus, we viewed this appreciation with mixed feelings—while it was "good" for the Colombian economy, it was hard on the Hunter family budget.

Another contrast, and a sort of commentary on the imitative nature of Colombian development, I report with less pleasure. During a visit to Manizales,[8] I was served with a Colombian-produced instant coffee

—which I dislike intensely as a substitute for "real" coffee no matter what its nationality or brand. And this in the heart of some of the best coffee land in the world! Incidentally, perhaps this is the proper place to describe the Colombian *tinto* custom and to indicate that there is much that we can learn in economics and otherwise in so-called "backward" countries. Practically all offices (fortunately including those at the University of the Andes) retain domestics whose task it is to regularly supply a *demi-tasse* of coffee at the desk of each employee. Practically every meeting is also accompanied by its *tinto*. This is a delightful custom and wise as well. Effectively, it eliminates the coffee breaks which can be so wasteful in poorly disciplined gringo° offices.

Another contrast worth reporting, even though not strictly a Colombian phenomenon involves education. Our youngsters attended Colegio Nueva Granda, essentially a gringo school but with substantial Colombian enrollment. This was a much better school than they attend in the professorial-executive-professional town of East Lansing. But the bulk of Colombian education at this level is in a deplorable state. One of my staff members was approached by a maid who had an opportunity to teach in a rural school. She wanted to learn how to multiply so that she could accept the job—at 250 pesos or about $36 dollars per month!

One common characteristic of countries such as Colombia is great inequality in the distribution of wealth and income. Great estates and great wealth are contrasted with the Tolima farmer (two acres) who told us that in a very good year he could buy a new machete (a universally used tool costing 3-4 dollars). Colombia is plagued by *latifundia* (huge estates) and *minifundia* (estates too small to support their owners or renters). I am reminded, too, of the Tolima widower (also a small farmer) who responded to our question regarding the availability of medical care. He noted that when he had money, care was available in the nearby town. When he didn't, "we just let them die as we did the mother of these three kids." The wealthy fly to New York, Boston, Cleveland, etc., for their medical care, although competent medical care is available in Colombia.

In a country undergoing a vertitable economic revolution in which the government plays a considerable role, one might find, as we do, considerable contrast in the policies of its government. Two minor examples of particularly wise policies are the following: (1) The cotton crop is sold to a single semi-official buyer. The farmer is paid only 90 per cent of the sale price until he demonstrates that he has burned the residue in the field to destroy incipient insect destructors; then he gets the remainder of the sale price. (2) Upon completion of all his training, a doctor is not fully accredited until he has served one year in a rural community. There may be better ways of assuring medical care in the countryside, but this strikes me as one useful approach.[10] Compare these, for example, with a price control policy on refined sugar which is not applied to raw sugar (*panela*), a basic ingredient in the Colombian diet. At times, the price of raw sugar rises to the point where sugar refiners sell their product to be remixed with the extracted molasses to produce *panela*!

                      ✿      ✿      ✿

Contrast—with other underdeveloped countries, within itself, and with the culture and economy of the United States—is the striking feature of Colombia and these examples could be multiplied endlessly. Those cited here serve to indicate their nature as well as to provide some description of the land and society.

# Political Trends

"Damn your principles! Stick to your party."
—DISRAELI

Colombian friends say that it is impossible to understand their country without understanding its politics. Herein lies considerable truth, and it is difficult for a foreigner to acquire sufficient knowledge to feel secure as an analyst of Colombian politics and other activities deeply steeped in political considerations. For that matter, this requisite severely limits the number of Colombians who can expertly interpret the country.

This sketch is intended to provide a taste of Colombian politics. For the student of politics, it will serve as a recent footnote to the excellent study by Vernon Fluharty, *Dance of the Millions,*[1] an account of the political development of the country in the twenty-five years prior to 1957. Unfortunately, Fluharty's account ends during the regime of General Gustavo Rojas Panilla, and the events following are presently of paramount importance. These developments are Colombia's unique contribution to political theory and practice and thus warrant considerable attention.

Colombians take their politics seriously. Colombia has two traditional political parties, Liberal and Conservative. Both are parties of the elite, although participation of the lower and middle classes is increasing. Both parties usually have been dominated by a strong man or by strong men. During the regimes of Alfonso Lopez (1934-38, 1942-45) and during the developing power of Jorge Eliecer Gaitan,[2] some liberalism crept into the Liberal Party. This gave the little man some political power and forced the government to take his welfare into account. This tendency was short-lived, however, and ended with the election of Conservative minority president Mariano Ospina Perez in 1946 (565,849 votes as opposed to the combined votes of two Liberals of 797,970).[3] With a Liberal boycott of the polls in 1949,[4] Conservative Laureano Gomez was elected president (1,510,619 votes to 25 for others with 501 blank ballots). His regime, at best, can be described as something less than liberal and it was he who was ultimately deposed, much to the relief of most Colombians, by Rojas Panilla.[5]

One observer notes, "The Liberal party began as anti-clerical, defender of the federal system of government and free enterprise. On the contrary, the Conservative party began as defender of the Catholic religion, of the central and authoritarian government and of intervention of the State."[6] In earlier years, marked differences in philosophy and policy may have been notable, but I queried a number of people regarding differences in economic policy and was able to find no great and distinguishing schisms. We, in the United States, can scarcely cast the first stone in *this* matter.

As already noted, politics is a serious business in Colombia. Virtual civil war broke out during the Ospina regime (1946-1950) and some two hundred to three hundred thousand people were killed in the following few years. Whole areas of farm lands were abandoned because of the conflict. Violence still persists in certain localities, but much of this appears to be more banditry and "adult delinquency," perhaps born of this period, than political warfare. Liberals warred on the incumbent Conservatives and vice versa. Cross-party marriages are even now rare although the old antagonisms may be disappearing. In road-poor Tolima, the very able Secretary of Public Works told us how it was recently necessary to build a second road to a certain Conservative town. Its other road, unfortunately, passes through a Liberal town, and too many Conservatives were killed on their way out of the mountains. Not all is yet peace and quiet!

Rojas Panilla turned out to be less than a blessing and was soon a hated and hounded dictator, partly because of his own activities and partly because of the people with whom he surrounded himself. As early as 1956, a series of meetings was held which laid the groundwork for the current *Frente Nacional* (National Front). A number of meetings established the principle that the Liberals and Conservatives could govern jointly through the device of the National Front. The principal characters in this drama were Alfonso Lopez, former Liberal president; Alberto Lleras Camargo,[7] former interim president and current president, and Laureano Gomez, the former dictator and leader of the Conservatives who was then in exile in Spain.

Triggered by student uprisings, Rojas Panilla was deposed May 10, 1957. Afterward, Colombia was ruled by an interim military government until the return of constitutional government in August, 1958. During this period, important steps were taken to establish the National Front.

An overwhelming majority of voters in a national referendum, December 1, 1957, approved constitutional changes required for the operation of the Frente Nacional. Two of these are critical: *alternación* (alternation) and *paridád* (parity). The former provides that the two major parties (all others are excluded) share the presidency on an alternating four-year term basis for sixteen years. It was anticipated that a Conservative would first occupy the presidency, but subsequent failure of the Conservatives to agree on a candidate led to the nomination of Liberal Lleras. Parity refers to the further agreement that government posts, elective and appointive, be equally divided between the two parties during this sixteen year period. This extends to government at all levels from ministries to *municipio* councils and to include even the deans in state supported universities. A further important (and now crucial) amendment provides that congressional legislation requires a two-thirds majority to "pass."

Elections for all elective positions with the exception of the presidency were held in March, 1958, and overwhelming majorities were returned for those who favored the National Front. After agreement by both party conventions, Lleras was magnificently endorsed by the voters as president-elect. His government took office August 7, 1958, for four years.

It took some time for me to learn the basic characteristics of this plan, to say nothing of its intricacies and implications. I was shocked when I discovered that the appointment of a dean in one of the departmental universities was restricted to candidates of one party in order to maintain parity. It was amusing to learn of Conservative *municipios* casting about for Liberals (long since killed or driven away) to fill their half of the election of municipal councils. I was amazed by the requirement that the president govern with half his cabinet of a different political party than himself. It seemed senseless to have a national congress and departmental assemblies divided equally between the two parties by *constitutional* provision. This made it difficult to see how the voters could hold anyone responsible for government action or inaction. I know of no other governmental arrangement which compares with this although it reminds one of some of the strategies of oligopolists and cartels in dividing their markets.

In spite of these doubts and questions, I became convinced that some such arrangement was the only way for Colombia to return to constitutional government with the forms of democracy and to restore a semblance of domestic tranquility. These things it has done; relative stability in the government has been achieved, and the National Front has survived for nearly four years. But the system contains the seeds of its own destruction, and it is doubtful that the Front will survive its full sixteen years.

The plan was desirable because of the nature of the alternatives. The government was left in the hands of the elite, however, and this elite has previously shown little interest in the masses. But the "little" Colombian could hardly have benefitted by a return to civil war between one faction of the elite and the other. Had the leadership been available, a Castro-type revolution might have successfully overthrown the existing elite of both parties and produced a revolution of the masses. This would necessarily have produced an elite of its own. It is not yet assured that the new Cuban elite will ultimately prove beneficial to the Cuban masses in whose interest it claims to govern. But this is not impossible and overlooking this possibility is both foolish and dangerous. In any case, no Castro was on the Colombian horizon to take advantage of the situation. One cannot help but wonder if Gaitan might have been such a person.

The legislative elections of March, 1960, demonstrated some of the difficulties for the future. In each party, slates were run of candidates favoring and opposed to the National Front. In this election, about 80 per cent of the Liberal half of the congressional seats were won by Front-favoring candidates while the remainder went to Liberals opposed to the Front. Conservatives, jockeying for the constitutionally provided presidential nomination in 1962, divided even more. Followers of Gomez, one of the system's architects, won only about half the seats while dissident Conservatives (followers of Mariano Ospina and Gilberto Alzate) won the other half. Candidates of a minor splinter group, delightfully referred to as *"fantasmas"* ("ghosts") also won a seat or two. This nearly destroyed the two-thirds majority required to pass legislation and makes the continued existence of the Front precarious.

The principal objective of the National Front was to reduce or to eliminate interparty strife, and it has been successful in this. But the effect has been to shift much of the conflict into the two parties as this is now the arena in which power is won. Intraparty strife became so physically violent that the Teatro Colón, one of Bogotá's priceless antiquities, was nearly destroyed during one party convention. Major problems arose with the Conservative party after the 1960 elections through the parity requirement. Each successful Conservative group claimed the right to "representation" under the parity provisions, and it was necessary for President Lleras to reshuffle his cabinet so that both the "Laurianistas" and the "Ospinistas" could share power. It took weeks to fill all the posts. Colombian cabinets resign *en masse,* frequently as a matter of convenience to the president. This permits him to replace those he sees fit without having to discharge anyone or even to ask for resignations. This mass resignation of ministers may or may not indicate some sort of crisis.

Colombia is not a federation of states as is the United States. The national government is strong, in an organizational sense, and the local governments have little or no autonomy. Governors of the departments are appointed by the president. Departments elect assemblies, but these are less powerful than state legislatures. Prerogatives are *granted* them by the central government and not *reserved* to them on a residual basis as are states' rights in the United States. *Municipios* have mayors appointed by the governors.

In the Spring and early Summer of 1960 the National Front was under attack on two principal grounds: (1) It was said that this unholy alliance of Conservatives and Liberals could produce no policy at all except one of doing nothing on important issues and of compromising on the unimportant ones. This argument would carry a good deal more weight if there were well defined issues between the two parties. It is true, however, that there is no room in this alliance for the extreme right or left. The only opportunity for expression of these groups is to elect anti-Front candidates under one party banner or the other. Such action is, of course, legitimate but success coupled with the two-thirds requirement can only result in legislative stalemates. The two-thirds amendment makes action on controversial issues next to impossible anyway—which of course is precisely why it was proposed.

(2) One party now claims to be the majority party (as usual) and is confident that it could win control of the government without any help from alternation. Politicians with confidence that they could win all in an ordinary election see little reason to guarantee the opposition a fifty-fifty split of the power and spoils under the Front arrangement. Present arrangements will be a continued frustration to that group most optimistic of all—politicians.

This has been a sketch of the current situation. As politics are serious in Colombia, so are they also volatile. The situation may change tomorrow. The National Front has worked and is working. Its future is insecure. One immediate and practical problem is the lack of a Conservative candidate to replace the incumbent Lleras. No one—of either party—can presently command comparable popular support. Contrary to the provisions of the planned alternation, Lleras was the candidate in 1958 because no adequate Conservative was available. Whether the Conservatives will abdicate their option a second time or insist on running a weak candidate is problematical, but this can be a difficult and dangerous situation in the coming year.[8] The likely alternatives to the National Front are so undesirable that one can only hope that it survives long enough to develop a more stable and logical successor.

❖   ❖   ❖

I wrote in 1955 from a more general point of view about the relationship between development, aid, and democracy.[9] Specifically, I was concerned then with those critics of the U.S. aid program who would make "democracy" or a "democratic regime" a prerequisite of assistance. This is still one of the major unsolved policy problems in reaching decisions regarding the allocation of U.S. aid so as to be consistent with ideological preconceptions, political realities, and requirements of logic.

There are certain necessary conditions associated with democracy if it is to be operational, that is, if the average person is able to exercise any real control of his political environment. A certainly necessary condition is a high level of general education. That such a social attribute is not a sufficient condition is demonstrated by German experience in the 'thirties.

Underdeveloped countries commonly provide a low level of education and exhibit a high percentage of illiteracy which is accompanied by (1) a low level of information and political awareness, (2) few media of mass communications, and (3) little sophistication about the problems confronting modern nations. No matter what forms of democracy exist and however desirable they are from other points of view, such conditions make impossible the realization of democracy in these countries— if by "democracy" we mean the continuous and direct participation of a high percentage of the population in the affairs of their government.[10] Arguments for democracy and the theory of democracy assume the *pre-existence* of an educated, informed, and sophisticated electorate. So far as I know, no serious proponent of democracy argues that he expects any random collection of humans (in our case to be chosen from an illiterate and inexperienced universe) to be able to govern itself wisely or well. Thus, general education is the basic underpinning of democracy as we know it even imperfectly.

Given this, what of the forms of democracy? Freedom of speech, freedom of assembly, freedom of worship, general suffrage are *per se* desirable in almost every case, but it is unwise to assume that the existence of these forms *is* democracy. These may be the very mechanisms used by the oligarchy to retain its power. They may even offer greater danger as invitations to demagogues for the manipulation and mockery of ignorant and helpless voters.

Thus, the allocation of U.S. aid and support is a complicated one for the idealist who would insist that democracy be a determining criterion. In the case of the underdeveloped countries, he must first shift from "existing democracy" as a qualification for receiving aid to the interest of present regimes in building a suitable base for the emergence of democracy. This may lead to the support of strong men governing *without* even the forms of democracy and the rejection of oligarchic governments ruling *with* all the forms of democracy. Basically, this involves motivations of rulers which at best are difficult to analyze—and one cannot wait for history to do it.

With this background, an examination of the educational base in Colombia deserves attention. In 1958, 37.7 per cent of the population over fifteen was said to be illiterate. Half of the rural population in this age group could neither read nor write, a startling comparison with only 21.1 per cent in urban areas. Significant differences between the sexes also appear. Fifty-four per cent of the rural females were illiterate while only 46 per cent of the rural males were so classified. In the cities, 24.5 per cent of the women and 16.6 per cent of the men were unschooled.[11] Little progress in this respect seems to have been made. Historical data show only a minor reduction in the proportion of illiterates since 1938.

For purposes of further comparison, illiterates over fourteen constituted only 1.8 per cent of the U.S. population in 1952. This is a striking comparison in itself, but as much is hidden by definitions of literacy as is revealed. In the United States, persons who had not completed six years of school were classified "illiterate." In Colombia, the determining characteristic is the "ability to read and write." In the census, competence in signing the enumeration form was *prima facie* evidence of literacy. Verbal affirmation of this ability was also accepted. The use of the U.S. definition in Colombia and more accurate enumeration would greatly increase the percentage of illiterate Colombians.

For the vast majority of Colombian children to whom any schooling is available, education beyond the five-year primary school is only a remote possibility.[12] A recent Minister of Education comments cogently on this situation:

"In Colombia, for example, we now finish 150 years of independence, with more or less 13 million inhabitants, of whom some 650,000 (that is, five percent of the total) can claim themselves sufficiently educated. Some three million remain with some three years of primary education. Six million and a few more are completely illiterate, and year by year it is possible to calculate that an average of 1,300,000 youngsters have no schools."[13] He continues, commenting much as I have done above: "This picture, based on the statistics, reveals to us in most clear fashion the anachronistic situation of a people which pretends to function with democratic instruments in its institutional arrangements, in its concept of the economy, and in all its ways of life, but which in its cultural affairs is practically in the same proportion and with the same concepts as lived feudal populations, crowned by a literate minority above a strata of semi-educated, and an immense human mass incapable of ascertaining the sources of its betterment."[14]

This is sufficient to describe the educational base on which Colombian democracy exists. It is not atypical among underdeveloped countries; we should not expect too much of it. So long as such conditions exist, we must expect governments of a "strong man" or of "strong men." Some are better than others.

✿  ✿  ✿

Fluharty insists that the rise of Rojas Panilla was due to a social revolution against the oligarchic Liberal-Conservative rule and that whatever else may have transpired from this epoch, the five percent would never again rule without taking into account the ninety-five percent.[15] In some respects, this now appears to be the case although Fluharty's idealized situation is far from realization. Rather, segments of the "ninety-five percent" have learned to make their voices heard from time to time and in various issues with results not entirely satisfactory. Some cases in point:

1. The elections of March, 1960, were a defeat for the National Front. The principal reason for the defeat is usually conceded to be the "austerity" program of the government, including "tight" money to reduce inflation, use of exchange to consolidate and reduce short-term debt abroad, substituting products of national origin for imports, exchange stability, a more or less balanced budget. One may quarrel with these objectives as means of approaching developmental problems,

but fiscal prudence is apt to be more successful in the long-run than is fiscal irresponsibility. Thus, assuming these policies generally wise, the voters can be said to have voted against their own best interest.[16]

2. The reactions of the little man are expressed not only at the polls. Shortly after our arrival in Bogotá, bus fares were raised from 15 *centavos* to 25 *centavos* (from about two cents to about three cents). In part, this was to permit proper maintenance (a large proportion of the buses in Bogotá were then idle because no maintenance could be provided), to pay for imported spare parts, and to provide something for amortization. Minor riots ensued,[17] and the government was forced (or felt forced) to retreat from its decision. A part of the compromise reached was that bus fares would remain at 25 *centavos*, but that employers would be required to add a wage supplement for the difference.

3. Colombia is further developed than its neighbors Venezuela and Ecuador in terms of diversification and industrialization. Colombia needs foreign exchange. It could (and does, as noted below) earn considerable exchange by selling to these neighbors. Many products, however, bear an export prohibition because of the notion that exports will raise domestic prices.[18] Only recently, leather began to develop as a substantial export; when this "danger" developed, an export embargo was imposed. One result of such policies, in addition to inhibiting industries in which Colombia seems to have a comparative advantage, is to encourage a good deal of illicit trade. It has been estimated, for example, that each year some $60 U.S. millions in goods leave Colombia illicitly through the little border town of Cúcuta.[19]

4. In May, 1960, the government permitted the cost of gasoline to rise five *centavos* per gallon, from about 14 cents to 14.7 cents per gallon in Bogotá. This led to strikes of all transportation in some of the principal cities of Colombia.

5. In Bogotá, meat, by U.S. standards, is extremely cheap. In part, this is due to price control established several years ago, and it has at least two implications: (1) Prices are not controlled everywhere; consequently a good deal of meat is diverted to other markets, and severe meat shortages are common in Bogotá. The control program makes no distinction between qualities of meats. Thus, the tendency is to deliver poorer and poorer qualities to the market as costs of production rise.

6. I mentioned earlier the ridiculous sugar-*panela* price control situation.[20] I talked once with the Minister of Fomento in whose ministry these policies are executed. He was completely aware of the economic

implications of such policies, but further indicated that the government could do nothing about them until the people had somehow been educated.[21]

7. A strike of bank employees all over the country occurred in August, 1959, and a more violent one in August, 1960. Such a strike is particularly paralyzing, and bank strikes have frequently been preludes to palace *coups*. Activity resumed only after the President of the Republic personally accepted the role of arbitrator in the wage dispute.

The above examples, in all their brevity, indicate at least two things. The oligarchy is still in power, but it has become much more sensitive to pressures from below than before. As the government has become more sensitive to the power of the masses, the masses have naively become tools for pressure groups to obtain ends sought to benefit themselves with resultant inconsistent and foolish policies.

*       *       *

One other comment is necessary on the Colombian political scene. Colombia has no "civil service" and this contributes to instability within the government. Partly because of the low pay of civil servants (a minister gets $3,500 per month or about $500 U.S.) and partly because of "politics," there is a high degree of turnover even at high levels of government. During two years, we saw three different ministers of agriculture—an average of one each eight months, which gave each barely time to learn the job. Each new minister customarily brings a few of his own "key" people who in turn appoint a few of their own "key" people. Thus, a change in minister or other official shakes a governmental agency from top to bottom, at least in its non-clerical functions. Under such a "system," it is difficult to develop long-range plans with policies having consistency and continuity.

Although one cannot obtain a complete understanding of the Colombian political scene from so brief an account, something of its flavor should be apparent. And it should be clear that politics dominate the Colombian arena and that prescription for economic and other ailments frequently must start with the political arrangements.

# Economic Development

"Do you know who made you?" "Nobody, as I knows of," said the child, with a short laugh . . . "I 'spect I' grow'd."
—HARRIET BEECHER STOWE, *Uncle Tom's Cabin*

The Colombian economy has already been described as a developing one. Complete support of this impression would require a more detailed description and analysis than is feasible here. First, it would require a precise definition of what is meant by development and what would represent an adequate measurement of this phenomenon.[1] Beyond this, it would require seeking and presenting data comparing the current situation with that existent two, three decades ago. Adequate and desired data are for the most part not available. There is, however, some statistical evidence in support of the contention that development is occurring.

In the absence of good data regarding the structure of an economy, an examination of the commodities it imports is revealing. Such evidence would be better if it did not also reflect changes in governmental policy such as has occurred in Colombia. Yet even with these changes, considerable can be inferred from important changes in the composition of imports. The following table indicates clearly the shift in dependence upon foreign sources for consumer goods to increased dependence abroad for raw materials and intermediate goods.

COMMODITY GROUPS AS A PERCENT OF TOTAL
IMPORTS, SELECTED YEARS[2]

| Group | 1925-29 | 1953 | 1957 | 1958 |
|---|---|---|---|---|
| Consumer goods | 43.5 | 19.7 | 8.2 | 7.9 |
| Capital goods | 32.2 | 38.2 | 22.3 | 26.6 |
| Raw materials and intermediate goods | 24.3 | 42.1 | 69.4 | 65.4 |
| Total | 100 | 100 | 100 | 100 |

The shift has resulted from several effects. (1) To some extent, previously imported goods are now replaced by Colombian produced goods. These goods may be wholly manufactured in Colombia or merely assembled there—or some combination in between. Prices in some cases are higher than when the goods were imported, but prices of other goods have probably been reduced. (2) Another way that this general effect was brought about was simply through doing without. Most notable to the new arrival in Bogotá is the almost complete absence of late model passenger cars. (3) While the first mentioned effect can be termed replacement by Colombian-produced "substitutes" (implying a high degree of comparability), other goods have been replaced with Colombian improvizations—products clearly inferior in quality or different in kind. Colombian rum, for example, has replaced substantial quantities of previously imported whiskey. (4) In a rather different categorization, one can also analyze the completeness with which substitution has taken place—it varies greatly from product to product.

The degree to which Colombia has become independent of foreign supplies of consumer goods was impressed upon me when I visited much poorer La Paz and found there in the store windows all the familiar U.S. brand names that I had not seen in Colombia for a year and a half. One clear effect of the import program has been to severely restrict variety available in consumer goods. Colombian woolen fabrics, for example, are good and inexpensive. Men's suits were available at about $30 U.S. and of good quality, but the choice of fabrics was small and the styles and colors very few. And this is as it should be—"variety" ought to be fairly low in the scale of priorities of developing countries.

A detailed analysis of imports is desirable and would tell a great deal. It would be even more valuable if data were available so that imports and Colombian production changes could be compared together. This would involve intensive study of thousands of items and cannot be undertaken here. The following table, though, of especially selected items is indicative of the sort of changes which have taken place.

These items are presented because of known developments in Colombian industry which has undertaken to supply the market with domestically produced substitutes. Not all products behaved in this fashion (mathematically impossible) nor can it be inferred that Colombia was "better" ("worse") off as a result of these developments. It is clear that important changes have taken place, and this is all the data are intended to portray.

Other data, less good but more directly applicable, relate to the occupational distribution of the labor force.

SELECTED IMPORTS AS A PER CENT OF TOTAL IMPORTS[3]

| Item | 1946 | 1957 | 1958 |
|---|---|---|---|
| Cigarettes | 0.7 | 0.2 | 0.4 |
| Radios | 0.4 | 0.03 | 0.03 |
| Light bulbs | 0.2 | 0.06 | 0.07 |
| Records | 0.1 | 0.008 | 0.0005 |
| Tires | 2.4 | 0.16 | 0.28 |
| Raw cotton | 5.1 | 2.4 | 2.0 |
| Cement | 0.8 | 0.06 | 0.4 |
| Sanitary fixtures | 0.4 | 0.2 | 0.03 |

These data are not sufficiently comparable nor is enough known about their compilation to extract precise conclusions from them. Most clear and perhaps most important is the appreciable decline in agriculture and the increase in manufacturing and artesan industries. Data in the service or tertiary industries are perforce less good, but if one aggregates transportation, commerce, government, services, and others in this general category, these sums result: 1925, 16.8 per cent; 1945, 22.8 per cent; 1953, 25.7 per cent; and 1958, 29.6 per cent. These give a rough guide to the kinds of changes which have taken place.

PERCENTAGE DISTRIBUTION OF LABOR FORCE, SELECTED YEARS[4]

| Sector | 1925 | 1945 | 1953 | 1958 |
|---|---|---|---|---|
| Agriculture | 65.8 | 59.9 | 53.8 | 51.6 |
| Mining | 1.6 | 2.1 | 2.0 | 1.4 |
| Manufacturing | 3.4 | 5.2 | 6.4 | } 19.9 |
| Artesan industry | 7.9 | 7.3 | 8.5 | |
| Construction | 1.8 | 2.7 | 3.6 | 3.6 |
| Transportation, etc. | | 2.5 | 3.2 | 3.5 |
| Commerce | 16.8 | 5.8 | 6.4 | 5.7 |
| Government | | 2.4 | 3.7 | |
| Services | | 12.1 | 12.4 | 16.8 |
| Others | | | | 3.6 |
| Total | 100 | 100 | 100 | 100 |

The last percentages cited assume special significance because to some extent the percentage of the labor force not required to produce goods (especially food) is regarded as an indication of wealth if not the degree of development. Lest we overlook the fundamental significance of some of these data, agriculture lost about one in five workers between the terminal years while the percentage in manufacturing almost doubled. This took place in an expanding labor force, so that in terms of absolute numbers these figures would be startlingly large for both losses and gains.

Existing national income data provide corroborating evidence.

PERCENT OF NATIONAL INCOME BY SECTORS, SELECTED YEARS[5]

| Sector | 1945 | 1948 | 1950 | 1953 | 1955 | 1957 |
|---|---|---|---|---|---|---|
| Agriculture | 38.4 | 38.4 | 40.8 | 18.5 | 38.0 | 37.9 |
| Mining | 3.4 | 2.5 | 2.2 | 2.6 | 2.9 | 3.1 |
| Construction | 1.6 | 1.4 | 1.5 | 1.5 | 1.5 | 2.1 |
| Transformation industry | 12.2 | 13.8 | 13.7 | 15.8 | 15.9 | 16.4 |
| Commerce | 8.3 | 8.8 | 8.9 | 8.5 | 7.8 | 8.1 |
| Finance, real estate insurance | 1.9 | 2.2 | 2.2 | 2.7 | 3.1 | 3.7 |
| Transportation | 5.5 | 4.5 | 5.6 | 6.0 | 6.6 | 6.1 |
| Public services | 1.4 | 1.1 | 1.1 | 1.2 | 1.1 | 1.4 |
| Services | 7.7 | 7.4 | 6.7 | 6.9 | 7.5 | 8.1 |
| Government | 6.5 | 6.5 | 6.4 | 6.3 | 6.6 | 6.1 |
| Rest of world | .5 | .2 | 1.4 | .8 | .6 | .8 |
| Personal rents, royalties | 13.5 | 13.2 | 12.3 | 10.8 | 9.5 | 8.7 |
| Inventory adjustment | | | | | | 1.2 |

These data can be made even more significant by combining certain items into secondary and tertiary industry groups, usually regarded as most interesting by specialists in development. If we combine transformation and construction as "secondary" industry, its contribution to national income production shows decided growth between 1945 and 1957—12.2 per cent to 16.4 per cent, an increase of about one-third. "Teritiary" industry (including transportation; public and private services; finance, real estate and insurance; commerce) increased its contribution from 24.8 to 27.4 per cent or about one-tenth.

The principal purpose of development is to increase income; for this reason, if no other, it is worth while to examine briefly the available data in per capita income.

These data must be presented with the usual warning concerning their reliability. CEDE had considerable interest in national income accounting. It was discovered, for example, that much of agricultural production is not presently included in the national income figures. A large part of such production is for direct consumption by the farmer and never enters into the market which makes accounting for it extremely difficult. Further, some products which do enter the market, such as potatoes, are marketed hapazardly and accounting for them is crude. After one session on national income, CEDE's staff was asked to estimate the amount that current national income figures *understated* the true amounts. Estimates varied from 7 to 75 per cent, the average being about 35 per cent. Thus, great caution must be used in reaching any conclusions based upon these data. They are next to worthless in making international comparisons of relative well-being and not good for reaching conclusions about absolute quantities, such as the percentage employed in agriculture or the percentage of income derived from agricultural production. Conclusions regarding the changes and directions of changes taking place within the Colombian economy probably are valid, however. This is the case, if for no other reason, because the persons who prepare the estimates probably would not present data which was inconsistent with what they observe happening in the economy.

PER CAPITA INCOME, 1945-1956[6]

| Year | Current pesos | 1945 pesos |
|------|---------------|------------|
| 1945 | 230 | 230 |
| 1946 | 274 | 248 |
| 1947 | 324 | 240 |
| 1948 | 374 | 240 |
| 1949 | 435 | 267 |
| 1950 | 507 | 244 |
| 1951 | 551 | 244 |
| 1952 | 592 | 279 |
| 1953 | 654 | 281 |
| 1954 | 730 | 282 |
| 1955 | 846 | 341 |
| 1956 | 829 | 304 |
| 1957 | 911 | 267 |

Per capita data are especially unreliable. Population is estimated on the basis of the 1951 census projected on the basis of historical rates of growth. It is likely that the birth rate has increased and certain that the mortality rate has decreased. Thus, population estimates for the years after 1951 are substantially underestimated. The price index used for deflating purposes is not a "cost of living" index as it better should be, and it probably is very crudely constructed. Given these shortcomings, conclusions regarding per capita real income are suspect. The data suggest a not very startling increase, and it is probable that they exaggerate whatever increase occurred. Yet, it seems likely that a minor increase of per capita real income did occur.

❖     ❖     ❖

The following is, in a way, a digression. It concerns statistical methods and is presented here to caution the reader concerning the unwary use of data from underdeveloped countries and to indicate further some of the problems faced by most technical "assistors" abroad. Statistics are a principal tool of the economist, and they are sometimes less than perfect.

It is axiomatic that underdeveloped countries do not have the resources to devote to collecting the statistics which they so urgently need. I have no idea of what the ratio is of fact-gatherers to employed persons in various countries, but if it is one of fifty in the United States, it must be one in a thousand in Colombia and perhaps one in five thousand in Viet Nam. Too many people are required in underdeveloped countries in producing the necessities of life to devote many of them to collecting data. This is as it must be, but the economic researcher in underdeveloped countries is continually frustrated by the lack of data, by the lack of current data ( *e.g.*, the most recent Colombian income data are for 1957 as this is being written), and by uncertainty concerning the reliability of existing data.

On at least one occasion I helped contribute to the world's stockpile of unreliable information. Viet Nam had just emerged from civil war, and partition by the 1954 Geneva Agrements left it with only the vaguest notion of even its population (the last census had been 1939). A group of us were charged with compiling the first national income figures for the then new country. One experience in this attempt provides some notion of the difficulties involved.

Rice is the principal product of South Viet Nam, and we arrived at its contribution in the national income figures as follows: (1) Total population was estimated and then broken down into three geographic groups whose rice consumption habits, we were told, differed. (2) Vietnamese members of the commission guessed daily rice consumption for one person in each area, and total consumption was then *estimated* by multiplying the *estimated* population of each group by its *estimated* per capita daily consumption. This was then converted to an annual basis simply by multiplying by 365 days. Summing the results obtained for all groups gave us estimated total national consumption to which was added known exports and estimated smuggling to give total production quantities. (3) This production estimate was then multiplied by an estimated price on-the-farm which finally gave the required value of rice production. As this is the principal product of the country, the results obtained were a major part of the final national income figure. About the only data in which we had any substantial confidence in the above procedure was the number of days in the year.

Some items in the income accounts were more easily estimated or counted while others were more difficult. As the work progressed, the group split into two, each making its own estimates. When brought together, one result was nearly double the other, and the final "official" estimate approximately split the difference. It was hoped by the U.S. members on the commission that the results would be published with an estimate of the reliability of each item in the calculations, but this suggestion was vetoed by our Vietnamese counterparts who wanted nothing to do with publishing official figures and then indicating that they might be less than reliable.

We partially justified this activity on the grounds that any estimate was better than no estimate and that we were pioneering and laying a foundation for future researchers. With such gross techniques, however, it must be constantly remembered that any changes over time may reflect (1) real changes in income, (2) improvements in data collecting, and/or (3) changes in estimating techniques. Further, politicians are not above manipulating such figures for their own ends. Certainly, in this case the exercise was a valuable educational experience for nationals of both the countries participating.

Two more anecdotes, these from Colombia, suffice to make the point. A U.S. official preparing to brief a group of visitors from Oregon and Washington, desired data on Colombian apple and pear production. He requested this information from the Colombian Ministry of Agriculture and was surprised to receive a time series covering pear production for a number of years. It indicated a neat and gently rising production throughout the period with something on the order of 37,000 tons in the final year. Converting this to bushels, it was found that this was about half the pear production of the United States, and anyone having lived in Bogotá knows that large quantities of this fruit are rarely seen in the markets. A further query to the Ministry brought a hastily revised and much smaller series, and by then my informant's curiosity was aroused. Investigation revealed that these data had been derived from a CEPAL[7] series which purported to give the total fruit production of Colombia (one of the most difficult estimates to make). An official of the Ministry had divided, on the basis of his personal knowledge, this total fruit consumption up among the several fruits. Thus, separate series were fabricated on pears, apples, grapes, oranges, etc., summing to CEPAL's total. Still a mystery is where the CEPAL series came from—especially when its several components are not known.

A very competent friend, once an important official in the Ministry of

Agriculture, told me this tale from his experiences. His boss once asked for an estimate of the production of potatoes (an important staple in the Colombian diet). In a few days, the supervisor returned to ask how the estimate was coming along. My friend had just about completed the design of a research project to make a reasonably accurate estimate. He reported this to his superior, indicating that he thought it would take about a year for the study to be made. This was too much time for the inquirer, and he turned to the telephone to ask his wife how many potatoes she bought during the course of the week. Converting this to a per capita basis, multiplying by fifty-two weeks and by the estimated population quickly produced the *official* estimate of potato production.

These examples are not cited as criticisms of Colombian and Vietnamese friends. They show a little of the tools economists overseas have to work with and caution the reader regarding conclusions drawn only from statistical analysis.

❀   ❀   ❀

The principal impression one gets of Colombia's economic development is the contrast between the old and the new—in a sense, its lack of "balanced" growth.

Some textile plants I visited (Sedalana, Coltejer) are extremely modern and produce goods of excellent quality at reasonable prices. I bought the best quality flannel slacks I have ever owned (they keep a press) for less than $10 U.S. per pair; first quality shirts sell for about $3 U.S. Variety in products is limited, but the textile industry has made great strides in the last decade and seems to be prospering.

Eternit runs a truly remarkable operation in the production of asbestos-cement products, chiefly roofing materials. This is a highly mechanized process. Its chief competition is tile products, still produced in much the same manner as they were in the days of the Spanish conquests.

Bavaria is a vertically and horizontally integrated brewing industry, modern and efficient. Part of its product is delivered to inaccessible parts of the country by company owned and operated mule trains. Incidentally, a few years ago, *chia*, a powerful corn homebrew, was outlawed by the government. As compensation for the loss of this cheap and widely consumed product, the government entered into an agreement with the brewers to produce a cheap beer not subject to tax. This agreement is still in effect.

Cemento Samper, near Bogotá, operates an impressive operation. Most startling is its transportation system. Located in the mountains just behind Bogotá, it must move coal up from the *sabana* and cement down. Further, it has to move limestone from its mines to its plant. These transportation problems have been solved by two aerial cable ways, one nine kilometers long to the metropolitan area and the other from the mines, twenty-eight kilometers.

A glass bottle plant of Peldar, Ltda., gives the impression of being technically efficient and well-run. Because of the shortage of paper and cardboard, it packs and ships its product in burlap-like bags. In contrast, though, is Vidrio, S.A., which made almost every technical and management mistake possible before its investment of some 10 million pesos was written off. Also in contrast is Cristalería Colombiana which produces various glass products for mass markets (but also including some luxury glassware) by time-honored (but no longer honored by much else) methods of hand blowing and shaping.

In the plains of Tolima, we followed a $30,000 U.S. mechanical rice harvester while in an adjoining field Colombians beat on pans with sticks to drive away the birds.

Thus, one finds modern, well-planned operations co-existing with small-scale firms using little and antiquated equipment. It is easy to jump to *a priori* conclusions about the inefficiency of the latter firms but this is a much more complex problem than initially is apparent. In the last decades, the United States has had an abundance of land and capital; consequently, most of our "efficiency" efforts have been to find ways to substitute capital (machinery) for scarce and expensive labor. It does not follow that this is efficiency elsewhere. Colombian industry provides many quaint sights, but they may make good sense where efficiency may require *capital-saving* in contrast to the *labor-saving* required in the United States. This kind of technological readjustment constitutes a major problem for U.S. industrial advisors sent overseas.

❖     ❖     ❖

Industrial operating conditions abroad are considerably different from those in the United States. Public utility services are apt to be insufficient and unrealiable, and it is not unusual to find that plants assume the responsibility for providing their own emergency water and power supplies. This adds greatly to costs of doing business because of the high fixed costs associated with producing a relatively few units of power. There are few firms in any one industry and limited productive facilities for any one product. Thus, the market for spare parts is small and must be supplied on a part-by-part basis from abroad. Costs of carrying inventories of spare parts are much greater than are similar costs for manufacturers in the United States. For the same reasons, plants of any size are equipped with substantial machine shops for repair and rebuilding of equipment to avoid, when possible, the delays and bother of importing replacements. These, too, contribute to costs.

In rural areas, companies must provide even more. I visited one oil production camp. In addition to the machine shops, huge inventories, and certain public services, this company had had to construct its own roads, housing for all employees, provide a community hospital, staff schools, etc. That this *is* a remote area is attested to by the fact that we visited a patient in the hospital at this camp who recently had been shot by the Montelone Indians—with three arrows!

There is a great deal more paternalism in Colombian industry than is now found in the United States. It is not unusual to find company stores (selling at substantial discounts) and company housing at well below usual rents. Partly, this is an effort to attract and keep qualified skilled industrial labor which is very scarce. Partly, it reflects the desire to minimize labor organization. This is also a way of increasing wages, in the real sense, without having to assume the burdens of the various social security programs which are related to basic money wages.

Industrial safety conditions are, by U.S. standards, appalling. In visiting the bottle works, we were led directly under the molding machine, and I expected that at any minute a glob of molten glass would drop down my neck. Even more exciting was a visit to Acero Paz del Rio, S.A., Colombia's steel mill. We happened to be there while the furnace was being tapped and were within a few feet of the operation. In order to see better, we jumped rivulets of molten iron in crossing from one side of the floor to the other. In the rolling mill, we also crossed the floor several times—jumping and dodging red hot iron bars as they were plummeting from one end of the floor to the other in the rolling process. In neither case was there any particular evidence that the companies were more careful with their employees than with their visitors. Our guide at Paz del Rio indicated that the industrial accident rate there was "pretty high."

Paz del Rio deserves a special study in itself, both as a steel operation and as a development project. It is something less than a complete success, at least in terms of expectations for it. It is nominally a private concern, but it was set up with government instigation and funds. Its current financing is unique—at least in my experience. Persons who have income of a certain level for income tax purposes are given an option: they may spend an additional four per cent of their taxable income for Paz del Rio stock at $10 per share or pay the same amount in income surtax. This is not a hard (if unhappy) choice to make as the stock sells at $1.80 per share and there is no market at all for surtax receipts. Paz del Rio is now experiencing what frequently happens to governmental excursions into business. Expansion and diversification are the remedies being applied to its difficulties. This may turn out all right, but considerable skepticism at this point is justified.

In most respects the whole field of industrial relations has yet to be developed. Unions exist, but their role in the economy is neither understood nor defined. Too frequently, as in other places, occasional abuses by union leaders have led to discrediting the whole labor movement. Many Colombians, as with some gringos, consider unionism as being synonymous with communism, and a great deal of education is needed on both sides. The labor market is the single most important market in any economy, both by reasons of size and the nature of the service being bought and sold. But there has been less interest in the labor market in Colombia than in any other of the "special fields" in economics. Collective bargaining, grievance procedures, normal union-management relations are not at all well developed. All too frequently, settling labor disputes becomes the task of the government. In 1959, for example, a strike of bank employees was settled only after the President personally agreed to arbitrate the dispute. Frequently, one reads of the Minister of Labor dashing off to try to settle some strike. Government officials have enough to do without having also to bear the onus of settling happily or equitably a series of labor disputes, large and small. Inevitably, too, this responsibility affects and is affected by the political problems of the day, already complicated enough.

Another full study should be given to the Colombian social security system (*prestaciones sociales*). If Colombia is an underdeveloped country, one might say that its system of social security is overdeveloped. I discovered this in making up my first budget when I was advised that to my salary figures I should add one-third for social benefits. This third covers a great raft of things—among them medical care, severance pay, industrial accident insurance, pregnancy benefits, annual bonuses, and retirement insurance (happily called *jubilación*).

The system attains something less than perfection, especially in regard to the medical services provided. It covers only a small portion of the total workers and is complicated to administer in a country in which administrative personnel is already scarce.

The complexity of labor law has one redeeming feature—as we found out after one of our maids had quit. Neither the maid or I understood the law, and within three days after her leaving, I was summoned into the labor court to settle my account with her. The lawyer explained my responsibilities under the law to both of us. On our agreement that he was correct, I paid the computed sum and the case was closed. Tens of thousands of cases such as these are settled for small amounts each year without fuss or bother; this system is certainly a great boon to the little fellow, especially if he works in a non-union shop. If there is not agreement between the disputants in these cases, then they go to regular courts and follow normal procedures. With this aspect of the Colombian labor law, I was impressed.

A minimum wage law is a part of the basic legislation as well. The minimum wage, to return once more to the importance of geography, is based partly on altitude. This is on fairly logical grounds that costs of living vary at least partly with temperature. The minimum wage is also based partly on the size of the firm for whom the employee works on the ground that big firms can afford to pay more per hour than can little firms. This legislation and the manner in which certain income taxes are collected has led to fictitious divisions of essentially integrated processes into a series of separate corporate identities.

Almost more than anything else, one feels the lack of technically qualified personnel in Colombia. This is especially apparent at the executive levels in both business and government. Young and inexperienced persons are finding themselves in positions of great responsibility because frequently they are the best available. In many of the plants visited, we found young men with one or more degrees from abroad as managers. They have great responsibilities and would be junior executives or in training programs in U.S. industry. One graduating Colombian engineer expressed considerable discomfort when faced with returning to a responsible position in Colombia and indicated that he was going to miss the early formative and learning years of his career which were available to young gringo engineers. Generally, the same prevails in the government; a returning B.A. in economics frequently is given a post of more responsibility than we would give to someone who had just finished his Ph.D. This shortage is in part responsible, too, for centralizing decision-making much more than in U.S. government and industry. That is, while the present plant managers have more responsibility than we would be willing to grant a person with similar training and experience, the position of plant manager, for example, has considerably less autonomy than is the case in the United States. Delegation of authority is considerably less, and the experience of having to go to the "top" to get firm decisions on even minor points frustrates the gringo especially if he does not understand the reasons for it.

*         *         *

Much of Colombian industrial development in the last decade has taken place through various policies of "import substitution," a term somehow thought to be different from or at least more palatable than "protection." Development has, in some other cases, come about through direct or indirect subsidization. Preferential exchange rates for industries deemed desirable represent indirect subsidies. Cotton, purchased at prices substantially above the world market price, is an example of the direct subsidy. Ten to fifteen years ago, almost all the cotton was imported, causing considerable drains on foreign exchange. Under the promotion policy of the Instituto Fomentario de Algodon, domestic production has soared, and in 1960 a minor "surplus" was produced.

It is difficult to evaluate the import substitution program in its totality partly because we do not know what "might have been" if other policies had been followed and partly because the program has not yet been terminated. Much of the subsidization has been and could be justified on the basis of the "infant industry" argument—i.e., protection against developed foreign industry is justified while an industry is establishing itself. Many Colombian industries are still presumably in this "infancy" stage. Only when they leave this stage, lose their protection, and are still able to compete with foreign products do we have the classical justification of their protection. If protection is not subsequently removed, whether the industry becomes competitive with foreign production or not, the program will have resulted in continued consumer subsidization of the protected industries. Then, justifying the policy becomes much more difficult, if indeed it can be justified at all.

Carrying out such a program involves hundreds of arbitrary decisions which implies adequate personnel for research, an adequate number of administrators, and adequate training for the administrators. None of these "adequacies" is present, and consequently many mistakes have been made. In an "import substitution" program, it is extremely difficult to measure losses due to differences in quality. As well, the authorities have from time to time overestimated the ability of Colombian firms to produce so that imports were reduced or eliminated before domestic suppliers could fill the needs of the economy—a case in point, barbed wire.

The "efficiency" argument so dearly loved by international trade theorists is not so dearly loved by Colombians, and their experiences in trade as an international specialist in coffee in the last few decades explains their position. As are many underdeveloped countries, Colombia's economy is extremely dependent upon the international market. In 1957 and 1958, coffee accounted for 76.1 and 71.5 per cent of Colombia's exports, and for 1957, the coffee exports alone equalled 10.4 per cent of Colombia's computed national income. Thus, Colombia's imports are largely dependent on its coffee sales. It is desirable to diversify these exports somewhat, but this is difficult. Colombia has, as an alternative, adopted policies to reduce its dependence on the supply of foreign exchange through its import substitution program. One can argue, to some limit of course, that it is acceptable to "purchase" stability for the consumer even at the expense of some of the advantages of international specialization and "efficiency." World War II taught this lesson well to Colombians and other Latin Americans. The following table presents clearly the fluctuations to which Colombian trade has recently been subjected.[8]

In very rough terms, the "crude index of purchasing power, Colombian exports" represents the physical amounts of imports that Colombian exports would buy in each given year. Thus, after 1930, it was twenty years before Colombia could buy again the same imports in quantity that she could buy in 1926-30. In the United States, we tend to consider imports as either "luxuries" (things we could do without or produce ourselves) or as "strategic" materials (manganese, industrial diamonds, etc.) which we *have* to have. We seldom realize that the very things we produce for ourselves are regarded as "strategic materials" by other countries—vehicles, spare parts for all sorts of industrial equipment, agricultural and electrical equipment. Gringos frequently have little idea what it means to an economy (1) to depend in a large degree on the export of one commodity, (2) to have the commodity a major part of the national income,[9] (3) to be dependent

SOME ASPECTS OF COLOMBIAN EXPORTS, 1926-1958

| Year | Export value index | U.S. wholesale price index | Crude index of purchasing power Colombian exports |
|---|---|---|---|
| 1926/29 | 113 | 62.9 | 109 |
| 1930/33 | 72 | 48.6 | 88 |
| 1935/39 | 46 | 52.3 | 53 |
| 1940/44 | 59 | 63.1 | 57 |
| 1945/49 | 143 | 89.5 | 94 |
| 1950 | 242 | 103.1 | 141 |
| 1951 | 282 | 114.8 | 148 |
| 1952 | 289 | 111.6 | 155 |
| 1953 | 364 | 110.1 | 199 |
| 1954 | 401 | 110.3 | 219 |
| 1955 | 356 | 110.7 | 193 |
| 1956 | 328 | 114.3 | 173 |
| 1957 | 311 | 117.6 | 159 |
| 1958 | 280 | 119.2 | 160 |

upon sources abroad for major necessities, and (4) to be subject to the whimsy of the movement of prices abroad. The above gives only a clue to the suffering, frustration, and ill-will that such dependence engenders. The use of four and five year averages early in the period obscures the statistical reality of annual fluctuations, which are poor enough measures, at their best, of human emotions.

In the coming years, the United States must develop a considerable amount of patience, understanding, and statesmanship toward countries such as Colombia. As quickly as they can, these countries are going to try to divorce themselves from this overwhelming dependence overseas, seeking at least partial self-sufficiency in certain products which they have previously bought from us. They are also going to seek to find ways to prevent the prices of internationally traded raw materials from gyrating so hopelessly. In the latter, we must assist; in the former, we must accept trade barriers, domestic subsidies, import quotas *against* our goods without thought of reprisal and with understanding. Doing otherwise will invite international political disaster.

# V

# Economic Trends

"Change is inevitable. In a progressive country change is constant."
—DISRAELI

"Change is not made without inconvenience, even from worse to better."
—RICHARD HOOKER

One of my principal impressions is that the Colombian economy is under great *strain*. This is vague; but examples of what is meant will demonstrate considerable, multifaceted stress. The impression is not that the economy is straining on all fronts ready to burst forth into a bright new era. Such an era may be in the offing, and the strain may be a forerunner of it, but it will not come about through a simultaneous explosion of all sectors of the economy into new, increased productivity. Allusion to this strain was, in a sense, implicit in describing the structural changes that have been and are taking place. These require radical changes in the historical structure of the economy and indeed the society, and it is not unexpected that changes of this kind produce stress and strain. We now turn to a discussion of specific points of strain.

Urbanization, for example, has taken place at a rapid rate. An estimated 15 per cent of the total population lived in the fifteen departmental capitals in 1938; this figure had increased to 21 per cent of the substantially increased population of 1951. Cali, Bucaramanga, Medellín, and Bogotá showed the most remarkable rates of growth with increases of 83, 63, 61, and 54 persons per 1,000 inhabitants per year. It is possible that these rates have increased, but even if they have not, this means a doubling of population in less than eight years for the first three cities, and for Bogotá, in less than thirteen years. As one would expect, all sorts of stresses have occurred from these developments. Public utilities have been stretched to, and beyond, reasonable limits. Housing is short, utilities inadequate, streets when they exist are congested, marketing facilities have not expanded rapidly enough to supply continuous flows of even vital commodities, urban transportation is terribly crowded, *etc., etc.*

Electric power merits discussion in more detail. Many industries, as already noted, provide all or a part of their own power. In fact, one such produces a surplus which it sells to the city of Bogotá. Existing "public" public utilities simply have not been able to supply increasing consumer and industrial needs. Bogotá has a rated voltage of 150 volts, but seldom if ever reaches this because of excessive loads. This uncertain voltage, itself, imposes considerable cost to both the house-holder and businesses. For all appliances and equipment requiring constant voltages, expensive constant-output transformers are required —to say nothing of the transformers required to reduce the rated 150 volts to 110. Because of dependence on hydroelectric power and inade-quate storage facilities for water, at certain times of the year both water and electricity are rationed—simply by shutting off in rotation supplies of both to certain sections of the city. Ibagué, a city of some 125,000, has lights so dim at night that it is almost impossible to read—a city of perpetual "brown out." Utility rates are low and controlled, which contributes to the difficulty of expansion of capacity. A distribution network does not exist; the principal cities have indepen-dent power facilities. In rural areas, electricity is found only in the villages, if there, and these depend on gasoline or diesel generators which usually provide power only at night.

There are individual stresses, as well as collective ones, involved in the shift of population from rural areas to the cities. This is a vast relatively unexplored area for sociological and psychological research. It is doubtful that conditions are better in the cities for the migrant poor, and perhaps they are worse. Educational facilities may be no better, medical care is more abundant, but it is not certain that it is more readily available to *these* people. Housing conditions are poor and crowded, and health hazards are probably as great if not greater than they were on the land the people left. They may have to walk as far to get water as they did at "home." Recreational facilities may be better, however, and there is probably a great deal more hope in the cities. There are no alternatives in the country, and in the city there are.

We know little about the difficulties of transfer of people from the relative independence of farm life to the industrial discipline of ur-ban employment in such circumstances, but the strain on the individual who leaves the farm to punch a time clock and to submit to the supervision of a foreman and to the boredom of repetitive tasks must be great. We have a great deal to learn about personnel relations under such circumstances.

As Colombia develops, it is becoming more interdependent region-ally. And as urbanization has taken place, it has been necessary for a greater proportion of agricultural production to find its way to the cities. This has increased the requisites for interregional and local commodity transportation. Road and rail facilities can yet only be described as grossly inadequate for the requirements of an integrated economy even though considerable progress has been made in the last decades. Continual emphasis will have to be given to improvement of these facilities for years to come.

Paradoxically, the trucking industry was temporarily overexpanded during our stay in Colombia, and truckers were being forced to give rebates from the established tariffs in order to compete with each other. This is one of the characteristics of rapid development—all sorts of errors in rates of expansion in dependent industries and services. One probably should regard this as a cost of development which should be accepted. The alternatives are both unpleasant and probably development inhibiting. Should the government seriously try to limit the expansion of an industry, there is little reason to believe that it would be better qualified to judge requirements than the private firms. The necessary controls to eliminate waste would inhibit development rather than promote it. Excess capacity, such as in the trucking industry, is temporary; and there can be no complaint about cheap transportation even at the expense of loss to truckers.

Modernization of the economy is involving transformation of its marketing system, and this will undoubtedly cause severe stress because so much of Colombia is now a nation of shopkeepers. In thirty small blocks of one poor *barrio* (neighborhood) we counted some 130 *tiendas*, small shops run by the resident family in the front room of the house. Generally, these shops stock a standard list of staples: rice, potatoes, cigarettes, beer, soft drinks, etc. These are not communal pools of refrigeration as most establishments do not handle perishables with the exception of eggs. Specialized shops sell meat and others sell milk. At once, these small stores are evidence of disguised *urban* unemployment and a terribly wasteful method of consumer distribution. As one moves from poor sections, there are fewer and fewer minute retailers; they are being displaced by supermarkets, chains of stores of the "ten-cent-store" variety, and general merchandise stores led by Sears, Roebuck and Company.

Agriculture, the most important sector of the Colombian economy, teems with strains of various kinds. Without describing Colombian agriculture[1] in detail, several of these are discussed below. Colombia is poorly organized to make the most of its agricultural resources. *Latifundistas* control large quantities of the most valuable land (i.e.

land in the valleys) and cultivate it very extensively, in cattle instead of crops. Small operators were thus driven to the hill and mountainsides.

This pattern is a serious obstacle to Colombia's development. It orginated with the conquistadors when native holdings were sequestered and the Indians left with only the poorer land. Inflation and tax laws made it possible to hold good agricultural lands profitably as an investment without resorting to serious farming to produce income. Only to a limited extent is this pattern passing. One does observe cattle grazing in the upper reaches of the Savanna of Bogotá with wheat, barley, and potatoes growing in small plots on the surrounding mountainsides. On the other hand, observation in the plains of Tolima and the Valle del Cauca reveals large areas devoted to sugar, rice, and cotton.

The problems of *minifundia* are still severe and involve hundreds of thousands cultivating small plots of marginal and sub-marginal lands largely on a subsistence basis (except for small coffee growers). There is a considerable pressure for land reform, and most elements even in the oligarchy recognize that it must come. There is considerable doubt, however, about the form it should take and how it should be brought about. In any case, it will be an immensely complicated proposition, trying to solve the problems of *latifundia* and *minifundia* at the same time, to say nothing of taking account of the structural changes going on within agriculture itself—especially that of shifts from small subsistence operations to large scale, mechanized commercial crop production of cane, rice, cotton, and barley.

Some of the stresses in agriculture are inherent in the above description, but comments on several are required. As already indicated, Colombian agriculture is shifting from subsistence to commercial agriculture, if for no other reason, because the increased percentage of urban population has to be fed. Marketing channels have not yet developed accordingly, and one of the most obvious faults is the lack of organized storage facilities. Potatoes, an important staple, alternately become a glut on the market and scarce. An expert in potato culture with the Rockefeller Foundation group asserted that no one thing would improve the lot of potato production and consumption more than the development of adequate storage facilities. By way of footnote, whoever establishes such a system will be publically accused of being a "speculator" even though speculations will, in the light of cold analysis, provide a beneficial smoothing out of prices through the year. Small producers, because of their ignorance of markets and lack of mobility, are frequently subject to the exploitation of middle men who frequent the local market to buy such commodities as eggs, corn, beans, etc., for later transport to the urban markets. How much of this monopsonistic exploitation exists is unknown; we made some attempt to investigate this in a study of potato marketing in the Bogotá area without much success.[2]

Agriculture is now changing drastically in certain areas and respects, *e.g.*, cotton and rice production. Largely this is in the hands of a few far-sighted "entrepreneurial" landowners. But the mechanism for transmission of the techniques and knowledge necessary to benefit small farmers does not exist. Rural education, even at the primary level, is too nearly nonexistent. Little in the way of agricultural extension is done. Education for agriculture at all levels has, until very recently, been seriously neglected although agriculture is the principal business of the country.

Considerable "surplus" coffee is produced, and Colombia can hardly turn to the United States for advice in solving this problem. This is a long-run enigma which hangs over the Colombian coffee scene, and which must somehow be solved. It is particularly perplexing because of the organization of coffee production which makes it difficult to convert present productive facilities to any other commercial use. Coffee is a mountain-grown crop. It has relatively high value per weight unit which can bear the high transportation costs to market as no other currently known crop can. It is paradoxical that the Federación Nacional de Cafeteros is the notable exception to those comments above decrying the lack of agricultural extension services. The coffee growers do have a fine experiment station and extension workers whose task it is, in part, to teach producers how to grow more and better coffee.

Certain areas of rural Colombia are relatively overpopulated while other areas, especially those now being opened up by new roads and the Atlantic railroad, are underpopulated. Reorganization of agriculture will involve consolidation of agricultural holdings into larger holdings and colonization of the new areas. This will involve tearing up of family roots, moving people to new lands which may be capable of producing only new crops. There will be increased risks, and any risks at low levels of income are capable of producing terrifying consequences. The fear of the unknown to the near starving explains much of his conservatism in undertaking new techniques and planting new crops. Failure or partial failure is calamitous. Agricultural reorganization will involve new schools, new commercial mechanisms, and probably continued governmental underwriting of risks. Again, we know little about the sociological aspects of these kinds of strategic changes.

The government's policies toward agriculture in general are at best ambiguous. Price control policies operate to keep farm prices low; and by attempting to keep city living costs down, both blades of the scissors encourage movement from the farm to the city. On the other hand, it is recognized that city living offers little if any improvement for the migrants and that it creates all sorts of social and political problems. Thus, certain priorities are being given to projects which will encourage people to stay on the farms. Inconsistency of policy, it must be noted, however, is no monopoly of the Colombians—especially with regard to agriculture.

Another important stress is observed in education at all levels. A later chapter is devoted to a discussion of some aspects of this facet of Colombia. It is sufficient here to indicate four major problems: (1) Few resources are devoted to any and all levels of Colombian education. (2) Education adheres to classical European tradition and is not producing "products" most needed by the emerging Colombia. In 1957, for example, of some 15,000 enrolled in Colombian universities, more than 75 per cent were enrolled in engineering, medicine, law, and architecture. Less than five per cent were enrolled in courses related to agriculture.[3] (3) Quality is poor at all levels. (4) Control is highly centralized in the Ministry of Education which reduces flexibility in adapting to needs of the new times. Included in these controls are "price" control of tuition charges of private schools which are the backbone of secondary education. These controls severely limit salaries which can be paid teachers thus reducing both quality and quantity of instructional staffs.

A great deal of the strain which has been described focuses in the government. A part of this strain is inherent in the peculiar political structure or system described in Chapter II, but much of its derives from the stresses of new problems of development and industrialization about which the government feels it must "do something." Part arises from the recent development of a new and vocal middle class. It comes also from the realization that something must be done in this era of "increased expectations" about age-old problems which were ignored or perpetuated by preceding governments. The success of Castro has created a suspicion that "it can happen here" or more probably "it *will* happen here if we don't do something now."

Strain ocurs because of belated recognition of problems and non-coordinated approaches attempting to achieve at least short-run "alleviation" ("solution" being much too strong a word). In this way, strange inconsistencies are allowed to develop. So little attention has been given to the solution of social problems in the past and so little emphasis placed on these problems that competent and trained personnel to develop and carry out imaginative programs is extremely short. The result is poorly qualified people formulating and carrying out some policies and the talents of those who are competent are spread much too thinly.

✿    ✿    ✿

Experience in economies such as those of Viet Nam and Colombia cannot help but impress one with the enormity of the task of development. Although this theme permeates nearly all the foregoing, two specific aspects are discussed here. One of them deals with the concept of economic development, and the other a specific requirement for development and some notion of its magnitude.

Economic development can be described as an attempt to increase the "happiness" of a group of people (usually a nation) in some defined or ill-defined time period. For "happiness," one may substitute "welfare." This is a fundamental problem and one with which philosophers have struggled since the beginning of time. The development economist by-passes this basic, fundamental question and assumes that if economic welfare can be increased, then the more general, over-all "welfare" of the subject nation will increase.[4]

But the term "economic welfare" requires further clarification. Professor Jan Tinbergen[5] gives an excellent description of its components. Economic welfare will be maximized when: (1) Production of goods and services is maximized. This is to say that people are happier with more to consume rather than less. (2) Equality in the distribution of goods and services is maximized. This suggests that a program which increases production in a poor country and allows all the increase to go to the already rich might even make the country "worse off" because the increased dissatisfaction of the poor might well outweigh the increased satisfaction of the rich.[6] (3) Stability is maximized. This is to say that people are happier secure than insecure. (4) Economic freedom is maximized. This suggests that freedom to choose among expenditures and between jobs makes people happier than being told what to consume and where to work. (5) Economic conflict is minimized. This asserts that people would prefer to have a given level of consumption without having to fight for it in wage and/or other struggles.

In cases of poverty stricken populations, greater emphasis must be on increasing production, but it is also well to bear in mind that these other maxima-minimum are important. Thus, "development" is complex even in its conceptualization.

A colleague and I did some computing regarding future requirements for Colombian economic development.[7] We projected population growth on the basis of historical data and assumed that the minimum acceptable (*i.e.*, "non-revolution causing") increase in income is 2 per cent per year per capita. Using the incremental capital-output ratio (the amount of capital it takes to increase income by one unit each year), we computed that between 1957 and 1975, it will be necessary for Colombia to accumulate some 35 billion pesos in new capital, an average of about $2 billion per year.[8] Over the projected years, this amouts to an average annual new investment of about 16 per cent of the projected gross national product. This is a greater proportion than achieved in the past over any considerable time—not impossible, but one requiring a good deal of wisdom, planning, and foresight. These calculations indicate only the general order of magnitude of capital accumulation required to secure even modest objectives.

If countries such as Colombia are underdeveloped, the theory relevant to their growth is even more underdeveloped. There is even some disagreement as to what development is and how to measure it. Without agreement on these fundamental issues, it is not surprising that there is less agreement on how the process takes place and how it is to be encouraged by conscious policy.[9]

＊　　＊　　＊

Several aspects of the process of development were particularly impressive in Colombia and Viet Nam.

Economic development is nothing more or less than economic history, insofar as we are concerned with the past. The economic history of a country or region is nothing more than a story of its economic development or lack of it. But even if development is an historical process, we cannot, in this day and age, concentrate on the past. Development is being sought, desired, and planned by many countries, and this puts a different light on it. Essentially, development is not something of the past but something of the future. One puts developmental planning and policy in its proper perspective to consider it a conscious effort, on a wide front, to alter the economic history-to-be of the economy in question. Of course, this is what all economic policy tries to do and developmental policy is distinguished only in the breadth and profundity of the changes envisaged. This is the proper view of the matter, and it should cause considerable humility among "developers."

There are several implications to viewing development in this fashion. (1) Essentially, it is a long term process. Immediate results cannot be expected overnight, and a good deal of patience must be exhibited.[10] This is especially relevant for taxpayers in "aiding" countries who do not expect a direct benefit from increased incomes abroad.

(2) It is frequently true that projects which produce the most startling results immediately will have less effect in the long run. An example demonstrates this point sufficiently. If certain resources for development are spent on the construction of factories to produce consumer goods, an almost immediate increase in consumer welfare may be registered. On the other hand, if these same funds are spent on the development of vocational schools, the results will be immediately less noticeable, but the productive capacity of the economy for all time will be increased. Unfortunately, the political exigencies of democratic-like governments are apt to require emphasis on the former type of expenditure.

(3) A whole series of almost impossible choices confronts us partly because there are so few analytic tools enabling us to see into the future and partly because we have so little knowledge of what people want. Suppose, for example, that two sets of policies yield anticipated results as shown in the graph. One set of policies will most probably yield income represented by Aa over the fifty year period. Aa₁ and Aa₂ indicate the most pessimistic and most optimistic forecasts as to the efficacy of this set of policies. Another set of policies (with its pessimistic and optimistic forecasts) will yield income as indicated by Ab. To complicate matters still further, the first set of policies will probably leave the economy of 2010 in a better position to increase its progress during the twenty-first century. It is clear, too, that the second set of policies yields a higher income during the next quarter-century. These are, whether we like it or not, the nature of some of the decisions which must be made. Rational choices are difficult, involving in this case the choice between more income for the current generation in the immediate future or greater income for its children and grand-

children fifty years hence. What family can make this choice, let alone what nation? To indicate that this is not just "theory," let us consider that the first set of policies concentrates on immediate expansion of productive plant and facilities ready to begin producing goods and services almost at once. The other concentrates on providing schools and education for the nation's youngsters, the productive benefits of which are not really felt for a number of years.

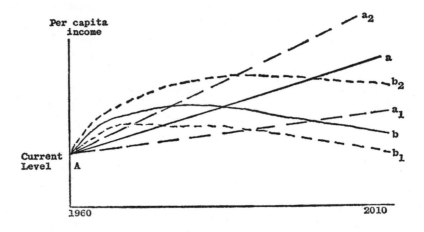

The essence of development is *change*. Dissatisfaction with current standards of living and with apparent prospects is the unalterable fact in these countries today, and it is change (presumably for the better) that they want. The kinds of aspirations that they have and the current states of their productive systems require *structural* changes. Of course, what can be done to increase output by shoring up efficiency in the existing structure should be undertaken, but great increases in production will require extensive revisions of and within their economies. A shift from agriculture to industry may be required, a change from *latifundia* to a whole new system of agriculture may be required, a completely new philosophy and system of education may be required, it may be necessary to tear the economy away from its international orientation. These are not repairing the chinks and painting an existing building, but essentially tearing the old one apart and constructing a new one. And, it is quite possible that no matter how radical and successful the surgery on the economy, it may still not be possible to realize the aspirations of the society. This, too, requires humility of "developers."

Change nearly always hurts someone. The invention of the automobile, which involved a structural change in the economy of the United States, was hard on buggy producers, producers of feed for horses, and the subsequent development of trucks has injured the railroads. Improvements in agricultural techniques have saddled us with the burdensome problems of too many farmers to be consistent with the relative prices they would like to receive. This recital could be extended *ad nauseum,* but the point should be clear. The process, as students of the industrial revolution know, can be a very rugged experience.

Two changes have occurred which make the problem of development in the twentieth century more difficult than it was in two preceding centuries. Governments are taking much more responsibility for development than they did previously. Thus, in a sense, development has became a "problem" when it was not so considered before. And as a "problem" someone has to devise suitable policies for it. In the second place, public opinion and action (including revolution) is stronger today than it was then. Something of a social conscience (or at least a "consciousness of the society") has developed. This social conscience requires that governments be welfare oriented and especially when their own policies are concerned. These developments have put governments in the unhappy dilemma of being held responsible as the prime movers of development (change) and at the same time playing the role of principal protector of the society from change.

This is such an important point and so frequently neglected, it is repeated in barest terms. Development is *change.* Change nearly always *hurts* someone. Governments are more and more forced to *protect* constituents. To absorb change, an economy needs to be *flexible.* A high degree of protection and security implies a loss of flexibility and makes the task of development greater than it otherwise would be.

It should not be inferred from the above that my conclusion is to eliminate immediate welfare objectives in favor of rapid development or to return to *laissez faire* attitudes of the nineteenth century. This is not, in any case, a feasible political option in most countries. It is well to recognize, though, that we are skating on a new pond these days.

Social consciousness has invaded the realm of public finance as well, and this will have its repercussions in development policies. Change implies risk, and when risks are high, any major dependence on the market mechanism to bring about development requires incentives. Many underdeveloped economies are sufficiently sophisticated to be imposing income taxes, at least on business enterprises. Treating all firms equally in terms of "fair" and "excess" profits may well reduce willingness of private enterprises to undertake new and risky ventures (e.g., those contributing to requisite structural change) with a subsequent frustration of developmental objectives. In such an environment, there is much to be said for the earning and retention of Schumpeterian profits in certain industries which particularly fill the requisites of development even though the profits they may earn may be by more usual standards "anti-social."

✻     ✻     ✻

As already indicated, the experts do not agree on what development is or how it should be measured. Experience in both Viet Nam and in Colombia has given my wife an infallible measure of the degree of development—the quality of servants available. In Saigon, servants were intelligent, even though unschooled. A post in the household of a well paying foreigner was about the apogee of aspiration for uneducated Vietnamese. There were few factories, offices, department stores to employ him. Colombia, in contrast, offers many opportunities. And the difference in what is left over to be servants is tremendous. This simply recognizes the emergence of a middle class as a part of the process of development—a class almost nonexistent in Saigon, but becoming very much in evidence in urban Colombia.

✻     ✻     ✻

A thinking social science technician serving overseas cannot help but devote a good deal of thought to the relationship of economic development in the history of the United States and what is happening and what can be expected in now developing countries. There are striking differences which make repetitious development doubtful if not impossible. We cannot expect underdeveloped countries today to develop in little images of the United States; indeed, it is doubtful that it is possible for them to do so however desirable it may be thought.

Even before the Boston Tea Party we were committed to the idea of general education in an extraordinary degree. Sufficient education was not available to everyone, but there was an appreciation of its value both for the individual and for the society. In terms of development, this meant two things: First of all, it contributed to upward social mobility of the individual. Enough people could and did leave the lower classes of society, at least through succeeding generations, that the frustrations associated with hopelessness did not become overwhelming. In much the same way, the expanding geographical frontier served as a safety valve (at the expense, to be sure, of the indigenous population) which permitted another escape from hopelessness. Second, this general education permitted the development of a real and operating democracy, responsive in some measure to the needs of the non-elite and preventing the total absorption of power by the elite. Popular education, the semblance of democracy, and expandable geographic frontiers have not been characteristics of those countries we now call underdeveloped.

In a fairly similar manner, the revolution of the British colonies in America much more nearly approached a revolt of the masses and middle classes than did the Latin American revolutions of the nineteenth century. These were generally revolts of the American-born Spanish against the oppression of crown appointed immigrants. Thus, one elite displaced another, neither of which were interested in the masses. Perhaps the revolts of the common man were postponed some century and a half and are now appearing in the guise of Fidel Castro and Castro's-to-be. The point is a crucial one. In the United States, we experienced a revolt by the people, a people which kept in its hands the product of its revolt, permitting the development of no semi-feudalistic elite. Revolutions in Latin America were of a different order, and most of the people in these countries have lived since then in feudal societies without hope, without geographical frontiers to run to, and without chance of moving upward in the social structure. These characteristics of Latin American societies are changing with industrialization and urbanization, and the elites are crumbling in some places and "running scared" in others. But the society is a different one, and the pattern of development will also be different. How graciously and how wisely the elite accepts inevitability will determine in part how violent will be the changes.[11]

The United States was fortunate in more ways than one in developing into what was almost a geographic vacuum. With population and other pressures, westward expansion was possible into a huge area. Because of wisdom or good luck, this area grew without the imposition of stultifying barriers to regional specialization and trade. The "mass market" became a reality and permitted the growth of industry to a phenomenally efficient size. These possibilities are not available

*I*

to presently developing countries except through such mechanisms as common markets and customs unions. Political and trade barriers are already firmly drawn, and to take advantage of the size of potential markets, some tearing down of these barriers is frequently necessary. The small size, both in terms of geography and income, of these national markets requires us to look carefully at the efficacy of competition as a means to develop these economies. One shoe factory in a country such as Colombia may be enough to supply the country's shoe needs. If competition were to be somehow imposed and another firm required, unit costs might rise because of the lower volume for each firm with the result that Colombians might find themselves getting no more shoes but at higher prices. With small markets, we can be much less certain about the advantages of competition especially when it is now possible to transfer the technology of large-scale production to such economies.[12]

The Wagner Act, federal income taxes, the Federal Reserve Act, the Pure Food and Drug Act, the Federal Trade Commission, Social Security, and the Sherman Anti-trust Act all date in this century with the exception of the latter, and most are less than thirty years old. These evidences of a "social conscience" developed rather recently in U.S. economic history. But most of the underdeveloped countries already have similar legislation—at a much earlier stage in their development. Whatever else one may say of the nineteenth century in U.S. economic history, the captains of industry and trade were generally unfettered in their developmental drives. There was unpoliced injustice, fraud, waste, but we built railroads, industries, markets, agricultural production. The profit motive, unhampered by income taxes and other restrictions, was no doubt a powerful force in the incentives for these achievements. If one believes in "capitalism," the incentives and possibilities of nineteenth century *laissez-faire* capitalism get considerable credit for motivating the real accomplishments of that epoch. The "liberal" measures of the twentieth century, desirable though they may be, impose rigidity on underdeveloped economies when flexibility is required and they discourage risk-taking when radical innovation is needed.

One example will illustrate. Excess profits taxation is used in some underdeveloped countries. This involves the notion that there is a "fair" profit associated with general classifications of economic activity —especially industry. By implication, profits over these are, to use a favorite Colombian expression, "anti-social." Such a concept of "fair" may be useful for the general run of firms in existence, but these countries need new firms producing radically new products and/or using radically new processes. Risks are high for these enterprises and "fair" rates may have little relation to the maxima required to encourage such production. The same argument is used in developed countries, but the urgency is less great. The effects on development of the "social conscience" have not received the attention they should have. One effect, I believe, will be to encourage more direct participation of government in what *we* regard as "private" sectors of their economies.

A great difference between U.S. development and problems facing underdeveloped countries today is this "social conscience" and *time*. We had no real social target, no example to look at and say that we had to "catch up". With modern national income accounting and with all the international contacts in this smaller world, people *do* make international comparisons of standards of living and the like. They *do* have targets; they *do* think that it is possible to improve their lots. They *do* think that the principal mechanism for doing this is their governments. Why should the peoples of poverty-stricken countries believe in *laissez-faire* or free enterprise or private capitalism? They have had such a system for centuries and still their standards of living are not much improved. Free enterprise may be the best *modus operandi* for them, but it is understandable that they are not now convinced. The United States must examine its position in this matter. It is not really "capitalism" we seek throughout the world, but attachment to the ideals of human dignity and freedom. Democracy and capitalism are by no means synonymous, but our foreign policy confuses them. As William Benton notes, ". . . critics from the United States become more doctrinaire about market economies the farther they get from home." [13] If we feel as a nation that capitalism is an important characteristic of present and future allies, we must be prepared to demonstrate what the system can produce under *present* circumstances and in the *relevant* economies. Further, we must be prepared to exercise considerable patience in the years to come as a whole new battery of economic experiments is tried by underdeveloped nations seeking to solve their perplexing economic problems.

# Perspective on Education

"Do you know, Carter, that I can actually write my name in the dust on the table?"
"Faith Mum, that's more than I can do. Sure there's nothing like education after all."

—PUNCH

My closest contacts with Colombian education are at the university level, so in descending order of my acquaintance, we first consider the teaching of economics. Higher education next receives attention, and secondary and primary schooling concludes our examination of the traditional complex. A new note of optimism is found in describing an exciting non-governmental experiment in education.

\*　　\*　　\*

Colombian university training in economics[1] exhibits these characteristics: (1) it is *not* training in economics, (2) it is carried on by underpaid, unqualified, absentee professors, and (3) it follows an antedated and unwise educational tradition. Most persons associated with economics education in Colombia are aware of its shortcomings, and substantial changes are being undertaken to improve the situation. This is most encouraging. My criticisms are severe, however, and deserve considerable explanation.

The teaching of economics is new in Colombia. Compared with law and medicine, it is still in its infancy as the first degrees were offered in the mid-forties. In June, 1959, when we made a study of those *facultades'* offering degrees in economics, two of the eleven were so newly organized that they had not yet produced a single graduate.

How is the training in economics *not* economics? It is a combination of "economics" and "business administration." This is partly linguistic accident as in Spanish *"economista"* is used to describe both persons specialized in economics and in business management. The basic difficulty, however, is not the language—differentiating terms could easily be developed. Rather, the subject matter is so new to the Colombian that an understanding of the distinct roles of these two areas of study has not been developed. Although this is an important distinction to make, it is not an easy one.[2] In 1959, courses offered by the eleven faculties of economics were classified (arbitrarily, to be sure); of 283 courses, 103 were courses in business administration, 85 were in economics, 43 in law, and 52 in other areas such as languages and mathematics. This compilation has hidden significance because the curricula of Colombian students include almost no electives; that is, the "mix" referred to above is a required one and does not permit the student to avoid "economics" courses to specialize in "business" courses or *vice versa*.

The principal result of this mixture of objectives, courses, and students is that the universities are producing neither well trained economists or well trained business administrators although students have been exposed to four or five years of work in a combination of both areas of study. This is unfortunate because qualified people in both areas are needed urgently in the Colombian economy and because there is no opportunity at present for correcting the shortcomings of the undergraduate programs through advanced work at the graduate level.

Colombian universities in fact grant two degrees at the undergraduate level. Traditionally, a thesis and a comprehensive examination are required to earn the full-fledged university-granted title of *doctor*. These are in addition to extensive "course" requirements. Only about twenty-five per cent of the students who complete the courses, however, complete the other requirements and a second degree of *"egresado"* has come into being. This pseudo-title signifies that the student has met the course requirements of his faculty but has failed to meet one or both of the other two conditions for the doctorate. Dissertations have habitually been poorly supervised, and the market justly makes little or no distinction between the two "degrees." Nor do the universities make much distinction; many of them hire *egresados* as professors. The dean of one of the larger faculties reported that the only students fulfilling all degree requirements were those who wanted to do graduate work abroad for which the legal degree is essential.

Any evaluation of these institutions must consider the youth of the professions of economics and administration. The principal problem reported by all the deans was recruiting adequate staff; this will be the case for some time to come. At least in some measure, the quality of a faculty is indicated by its training. A compilation of the earned degrees of professors indicates: of 236 professors in nine faculties, fifty-five (23.3 per cent) had degrees in economics; seventy (29.7 per cent) had degrees in law; fifty-one (21.6 per cent) had some other degree; and sixty (25.4 per cent) had no degree at all. This is especially significant with the added notation that of these 236 professors, only twenty-six (11 per cent) had *any* advanced degree.

These data require some explanation so that evaluation is not more severe than warranted. Colombian faculties are much more self sufficient than is the case of the U.S. university "department"—and, for that matter, the "college." Typically, the Colombian faculty hires its own professors to teach whatever courses in English, mathematics, sociology that it may offer. This accounts for a large proportion of the "other" degrees in the compilation above. Secondly, a gringo interpretation of "degree" was used in making this study; thus, *egresados*, recognized as *de facto* degree holders in Colombia, were excluded from this category. This accounts for the large proportion of "no degrees." However charitably one views this, the fact remains most teaching is done in these faculties by professors who do not have the educational qualifications to teach in any reputable United States university. Poor staff quality is recognized by faculty and university authorities and, encouragingly, vigorous measures are being undertaken to correct the situation.

Consideration of the remuneration received by Colombian professors is also depressing. So few of them teach full-time that a meaningful study of salaries was difficult. Of 230 professors, only twenty-one were full time; most of the part-time persons only taught one course.[4]

A detailed study of the salary structure developed summary data which make the situation patently clear. In terms of actual salary, 186 of 229 professors received less than 400 pesos per month (*i.e.*, 81 per cent received less than roughly $50 U.S.). Some 221 (96 per cent) received less than 2200 pesos (about $275 U.S.). With dubious manipulation, these data were converted to full-time equivalent salaries for most of the group, that is, estimates were made for the part-time professors as to what they would have received if they had taught full-time. Of 209 for whom information was available and computation possible, 66 (32 per cent) would have received less than 500 pesos monthly ($60 U.S.); 100 (48 per cent) less than 800 pesos ($100 U.S.); and 194 (93 per cent) less than 1000 pesos ($125 U.S.). Even with a very large margin of error, these salaries are appallingly low.

Producing additional coffee requires about 4-5 years, the time for new bushes to mature. "Producing" professors requires an even longer gestation period. Immediately increasing salary scales would not materially affect the numbers of qualified people available for teaching positions. Consideration is being given to making professorships attractive enough to attract and hold good people and to encourage them to seek better professional qualifications, but only modest progress has been made. In any case, improved quality is far more important in the long-run for Colombian faculties than is increasing the number of professors.

Poor use of existing staff wastes these already scarce resources. In one university, for example, third-year students were required to attend classes thirty-six hours weekly. They were listening to lectures continually and doing little advance preparation for classes, not to mention independent study. The amount of absorption from the last six hours of those classes must have been nil. It is a legitimate criticism of university education that the student does too little for himself, but Colombian education even exceeds the U.S. propensity to spoon-feed.

There are several reasons for scheduling classes so extensively. In the first place, and perhaps most important, this is traditional; people would suspect a program that kept students in class only about eighteen hours per week, a figure generally regarded as excessive in the United States. Colombians more frequently cite the undisputed fact that libraries are poor and books difficult for students to buy as reasons for not requiring students to do much outside the classroom. There is merit in these arguments, but not nearly enough, and the wrong conclusions are drawn from them. Rather, the following could be done with greatly improved educational opportunities. Suppose a faculty has a teaching budget which includes the equivalent of six full time professors (6 professors x $1,000 per month x 12 months = $72,000). By halving its contact hours, it could "save" $36,000. Half these savings devoted to library acquisitions would more than triple the typical faculty's present annual library budget and would permit using the other $18,000 to increase by 50 per cent salaries in the remaining three professor positions. Still another reason for such full weekly schedules is related to the teaching format which is discussed in the following paragraph.

It has already been indicated that much of the teaching is by part-time professors. Typically, the part-time professor teaches only one class and that at a terminal hour of the day[5] so as to interfere as little as possible with his job. This job is his primary source of income and and being a principal responsibility requires most of his attention. Depending on the nature of this position and his sense of responsibility to his students, the teaching job he does runs all the way from poor with a high degree of absenteeism to excellent. The Colombian professor does no university related research and produces no scholarly publications—unless of course research and publication are related to his prime position. He is fortunate if he has an opportunity to keep up with developments in his teaching field. He has little time to prepare for courses to include a plan of assigned readings for the semester and supervision of independent student work. He comes to the university only during teaching hours and is almost never available to his students. This, unfortunately, is the picture of the typical professor.

Certainly it is hard for the administrator-dean (typically part-time as well) to get the requisite cooperation, commitment, and responsibility from those who are essentially grantors of charity. I am not being critical of the professor as an individual; under present circumstances, he fills a void; and the fact that he fills it poorly is not his fault, but rather the system's. Some observers of Latin American education have indicated that such professors take these posts largely because of the prestige associated with them. By the favorite Colombian measuring device, *ojómetro*,[6] this generalization does not apply to economics professors in Colombia. Certainly, the evidence does not indicate that they take the position for money. Rather, most of them are sincere, dedicated individuals who realize the importance of education and are doing the best they can with a bad situation.[7]

There is, too, an unfortunate, but very natural tendency to concentrate training around available materials. Unfortunately for Colombian education, these too frequently are books written in the United States for U.S. students with little or no relevance to the Colombian economy or for Colombians. Imagine the problem we would have trying to teach U.S. students from books written in India for Indian students! In medicine, the natural sciences, and agriculture this is not a critical problem. But in the social sciences, where historical influences, legislation, social structure, value systems, and social institutions play such important roles, this shortage of adequate teaching materials is critical. The development of a corps of qualified and full-time professors will do much to alleviate this problem. This is clearly an area in which technical assistance from abroad would have long-run impact on a broad front.

Unless he can go abroad, the newly-graduated Colombian has no opportunity for the specialization and "seasoning" offered by graduate work. Further, the newly-graduated Colombian economist may assume responsibilities far in excess of those assigned the U.S. graduate. He may become, as I have seen many do, a chief of planning in a department, a division chief in a ministry, or assume considerable responsibility in the central bank. Thus, while most B.A. programs in the United States do not purport to turn out finished "economists," Colombian faculties are doing so, whether they are doing it well or not. Their responsibilities are far greater than their U.S. counterparts.[8]

This section on the teaching of economics is concluded with a brief comment on the Sociedad Colombiana de Economistas, roughly the counterpart of the American Economic Association. Two of its activities throw some light on the status and attitude of the profession. I attended one committe meeting at which it was seriously proposed that the society should petition congress. The gist of the request was to be a law defining the profession of *economista* to include the course of study to be followed to earn this exalted title. Another of its activities is to lobby in government circles, primarily with the objective of having certain governmental positions restricted to *economistas*. There is some merit in craft unionism, to be sure, but in such a craft as ours, fraught with political and ideological differences, an invitation to the government to define and limit the craft is most fool-hardy.

❊ ❊ ❊

Many of the problems of higher education in Colombia are associated with financing.[9] As might be expected, the principal financial problem is too little money devoted to higher education and to education in general. In part, this is due to the poverty of Colombia; by U.S. standards, its resources are extremely limited. By other standards, however, it does not rate among the poorest countries and could probably well devote a greater portion of its resources to this end. Although not a "monument-mad" country as are some other Latin American nations, it is not hard to find examples of governmental expenditures which, at least by my value system, might better have gone into education. One may draw the same conclusions from his religiocentrism about investments in churches and related organizations. Much of the responsibility for allocating few resources to education lies not in Colombia's poverty but rather in its traditions which regard education as a service to be bought by those who can afford it rather than as socially provided "right." This is still largely the case although there is evidence of a more universal approach. For example, student fees at the National University are based on the income tax returns of the parents.

There is no adequate means for determining the "proper" amount for a country such as Colombia to devote to education,[10] but some rough guide may be possible. Education is one of the paramount ingredients necessary for economic development. It is associated with political development, acquiring the requisite technical proficiencies, increasing the mobility of the factors of production, increasing production on small agricultural holdings, reaching a level of intellectual sophistication where appropriate developmental policies can be explained to the people. The importance of education increases as development is considered as an historical process occurring in decades and generations rather than in months and a few years.

In establishing a rule of thumb, it is assumed that the objectives include attaining rates of growth at least equal to those of the more advanced countries. This is assumed because a substantial amount of authority accepts the notion that even though these countries may become "better off" in absolute terms that they will really feel "worse off" if they lose ground in relative terms. That is, if the rate of growth in Colombia is 2 per cent per year while that of countries with whom she compares herself is 4 per cent, she may feel that she is actually losing ground. Thus, Colombia ought to be spending at least as great a percentage of its income for education as the more advanced countries. This is only a very rough approximation, but it indicates the magnitude of the problem. In a most crude comparison, the United States spent about 4 per cent of its national income on education in 1956; Colombia devoted about 1 per cent of its national income for this purpose the following year. Although no neat, constant relationship between expenditures on education or growth are hypothesized, it is not unreasonable that Colombia should set 4 per cent of her national income (a 400 per cent increase!) as a rough target.

Granted that expenditures on higher education are too low, there is still room for improvement in existing allocations. As suggested above, the requirement of fewer classes could free resources for expanding libraries and higher faculty salaries at no loss to the quality of education. Especially in economics and perhaps in other subjects, universities are now too competitive and duplicate facilities for too few students. In the study of the teaching of economics, we found many classes being taught for five-ten students. This is wasteful in the extreme of both money and very scarce teaching resources. Small entering classes and a very high rate of attrition—most of which universities blame on inadequacies in the secondary schools—are responsible.

Another possibility for internal economies lies in reducing the self-sufficiency of the faculties and developing the idea of "service departments" and "service courses." Law faculties teaching economics and each organization hiring its own English and mathematics teachers is wasteful in terms of scarce teachers and money. A far-sighted and more extreme proposal made by one of the rectors suggested that each university should concentrate on the first two years of training in most disciplines and in only very few areas for the final two or three years. Thus, a student would study at the nearest university for two years before migrating to that university specialized in the discipline of his choice. This would at once permit a better development of programs, avoid expensive duplication, and permit instruction to be presented to a more economical number of students. More attention should be given to specialization among the universities and to some form of "college preparatory" course in order to salvage potentially good students who fail in the first year or so due to inadequate preparation.

As already indicated, professorial salaries are so low that it is impossible to select teaching as a career. There are few exceptions: the independently wealthy who may or may not be good teachers and the fewer extremely dedicated and self-sacrificing persons on whose good nature Colombian education has no right to trade or to depend. Perhaps the most important effect of this salary scale is the absence of an independent community of scholars, conducting research and speaking its mind on questions of the day. Poor teaching is another significant result. Most universities and the government are now seeking ways of expanding overseas specialization of staff members and prospective staff members. This is a first step and an important one; but the staffing problem will not be solved until attractive salaries can be offered persons returning from these opportunities abroad. Contracts which bind recipients to university service on their return can provide only a year or two of service and cannot substitute for a competitive salary structure. Somehow the universities must find some way to make it possible for young Colombians to choose teaching as a career. When this is done, what are now comparatively minor problems will become more important ones for the universities to solve: establishment of ranks and, more important, clearly established criteria for advancement other than seniority. These latter two familiar paraphenalia of the U.S. campus do not now exist in Colombia; but in the present context, their absence is not important.

As most of Colombian public institutions suffer, Colombian universities lack continuity, especially among administrators. Deans and rectors (presidents) come and go, by choice and by pressure. There is no career in this area either. Again, by *ojómetro*, an average tenure of two years for university rectors probably exaggerates reality. This constant change of leadership does little to promote the long-run

growth and strength of these institutions and does a great deal to pre-
serve the *status quo,* which has little to commend it.

Tradition has manacled Colombian higher education.  Most Euro-
peans criticize U.S. education on the grounds that we treat university
students as, to be charitable, high school students.  We require a core
curriculum, certain courses are required, class attendance is required,
little independent study is required, exams are frequent.  Not only do
we run educational cafeterias, in the European eyes, but we spoon-
feed as well.  We complete the metaphor in finally requiring a certain
amount of regurgitation at examination time.  To whatever extent
these criticisms are valid of U.S. education, they are more so when
related to Colombia.  This is evidenced in the appalling number of
hours the Colombian student is required to be in class, how little is
required of him outside of class, and the emphasis on the lecture method
of instruction.  It is also important in two other respects.  The
electives permitted the student are very few indeed.  In part, this
is simply a matter of economy and reflects the fact that many faculties are now operating with too few students to offer alternatives to
the student.  Vertical orientation of the faculties requires that the
student choose his specialization on entering the university.  Coupled
with the self-sufficiency characteristic, it is virtually impossible for
the student to "shop around" seeking his major interest or to change
from one curriculum to another once he has committed himself.  The
thesis and general examination requirements may be thought to be
offsetting *desiderata,* but most students do not complete these requirements and theses have generally been poorly supervised.

Centralization is a problem throughout Colombia, and it is a
problem in Colombian higher education.  Until recently, Colombian
universities were directly dependent upon the Ministry of Education
for financing, regulation, and control.  Semi-independence has now
been attained through an organization of the rectors, but the Minister
of Education still has considerable control through, if nothing else,
his hands on the purse strings.  This control might be used wisely to
enforce a "non-competitive" policy among the universities, which they
ought to enforce themselves, but there is little evidence that this has
been done.  This centralization is also a severe strain upon the intellectual independence of the university.

Gringos are frequently astounded at the role played by Latin American students in national politics and, for that matter, in the administration of their universities.  Latin American revolutions have frequently involved students as major participants, and sometimes they

have been leaders. As already indicated, students were instrumental in the downfall of Rojas Panilla. Unfortunately they have been less successful in filling vacancies than in creating them, so frequently their objectives have not been ultimately satisfied.

A principal weapon of the students is the strike. We witnessed a major student strike at the National University which forced the resignation of its very fine rector, Mario Laserna. This began with complaints about professors in the architecture school and ultimately spread to all faculties, even branches in Medellín and Palmira. The whole University of Cartagena program was interrupted for weeks over some dispute in assigning quarters to some fifth-year medical student. Even high school students strike. Not only is student influence felt in this negative sense, but they have a positive voice in the formulation of policy. I advised one university concerning the establishment of an economic research center. One active participant in the discussions was a third-year student who clearly had to be satisfied as a member of the directive committee of the faculty.

What are we to think of all this? At the outset, these student interests and attitudes are refreshing compared with the more bovine behavior of U.S. students. On the other hand, it is considerable power in the hands of the inexperienced and immature. It is frequently said that the students are used by other groups (inevitably said to be the Communists) to gain nefarious ends. Some of their objectives arouse considerable sympathy, but not all are wisely chosen. With the high rate of student attrition, the average student tenure in the universities only approaches that of the rectors; with so little experience, they can hardly be expected to reach decisions in academic matters even in their own best interests. It is clear, too, that they have many legitimate complaints concerning the educational fare offered them, and some remedial action has been obtained through student pressures.

I discussed this at some length with a Colombian educator friend. He had just "survived" a strike threat of his students because he had failed "too many" of them in a particular course. At that point, he had no use for student autonomy and preferred the professorial autocracy of the United States. But later in the conversation, he allowed that the strikes he had participated in (led?) as a younger man had been for "good" causes.

Once the doors are opened to these kinds of student activities, there seems to be no way to limit them to "desirable" or "legitimate" issues. Perhaps many of these problems will be automatically solved as Colombian education becomes more vigorously undertaken and its quality improved.

Higher education presents a dark and dreary picture, but perhaps it is the darkness before the dawn. There are evidences of great improvements to come—some of which have been mentioned. Generally, administrators and professors recognize their problems which is the first step. They are beginning to solve some of them. Education in areas other than traditional law and medicine is becoming more acceptable—evidenced by the growth of faculties of economics in the last decade and the establishment of a new school of sociology in the last two years. In summary, Colombia is a developing country; her higher education is developing, too, perhaps at a slower rate and surely following when it should be leading.

*     *     *

It would indeed be surprising if one found an adequate educational configuration under so weak a university structure. There is nothing in Colombian primary and secondary education to surprise us in this respect—even from casual observation. In 1958, of an estimated population of 2,633,740 between the ages of seven and fourteen, only about two-thirds were enrolled in school.[11] If this were to read "regularly attending," the figure would be far smaller. In comparison, in the same age group, 99.5 per cent were enrolled in the U.S.[12] A study of some 230 small farmers, chosen more or less at random in the plains of Tolima (a not poor agricultural region) indicates that nearly 40 per cent had had no schooling, 58 per cent less than 2 years, and 92 per cent less than four years.[13] Educational opportunities, however, for the present crop of youngsters are somewhat better than they were for their parents. The data from Tolima, of course, are applicable to the latter group.

Not only is there a lack of education in terms of quantity, but its quality must also be sadly deficient. The one-room school is standard in the rural areas, and one can hear the sing-song chanting of antiquated pedagogy as one passes them. The reader may recall at this point the maid offered a teaching job if only she could learn to multiply.

Public school education is shunned by those who have any chance at all of avoiding it. The middle class family puts great emphasis on education and goes to great sacrifices in order that at least one of its offspring may have the opportunity to attain at least the equivalent of a high school education—in a private school. Snobbery plays little part in this selection; parents correctly feel in most cases that the private school is where the education is.[14]

Other than the general criticisms regarding quantity and quality, a tendency toward classical or traditional education is also noted. Particularly at the high school level, it would be wise to give much more emphasis on vocationally oriented curricula, especially on agriculture in the rural areas.

* * *

I first heard in Viet Nam of Colombia's Radio Sutatenza and its educational experiment. This is a most noteworthy program and careful consideration should be given to its objectives and methods by all those who have an interest in instigating change among the people hardest to reach, the peasants. The elements of this church-operated (and government supported) program are providing cheap radios, training instructors, and broadcasting educational programs.

The radios provided under this program are single band, battery operated sets produced in Colombia. These are made available through parish priests for 120 pesos; it is expected that people will buy them on a neighborhood group basis. Bright young people are selected from the parishes for special training and are taken for a three-four months course to Sutatenza, an agricultural mountain village about three hours from Bogotá. Here they are given an intensive course, designed to improve their own educational achievements and to train them in the instructional techniques used in the courses in which they will ultimately be assistant instructors. This is capped off with practical agricultural training for the boys and home economics instruction for the girls.

Most emphasis is placed upon the literacy program although this is by no means all that is done. The assistant instructors return home and then are expected to cooperate with the local "schools." These schools consist of a few adults who have banded together to purchase a radio, a gong for summoning the "students," a few training charts, and some cheap simple pamphlets. Literacy instruction is carried in the evening hours by radio, and the assistant instructor attends to answer questions, to point to the charts as instructed by radio, and to correct student mistakes. While this program receives major emphasis, other sessions are devoted to diet, simple animal care, instructions on crop improvement, home improvement, etc. All is pitched at the level of the illiterate, but not unintelligent, peasant. Officials of Acción

Social Popular, of which this program is a part, estimate that they have as many as a half million "pupils." Unfortunately, no serious evaluation of a sociological or economic nature has been made of the program. Its directors indicate frankly that they have no real measure of the value of the work they are doing; they do have, however, a huge file of letters written by persons just freed from the bonds of illiteracy which is partially indicative and surely is sentimentally very impressive.

Any program reaching so many people in a politically sensitive country has its critics, and Colombian critics object to past political use of the program, its potential use for political purposes, and its control by the church. Evaluating these criticisms is beyond my judgment.

This is a most promising technique and one which has demonstrated its ability to be a going concern although measurement of its successes are not concrete. It is impressive enough that I recommend its emulation elsewhere without further detailed evaluation although a sociological study of this project and its effects is an extremely rich and unexploited vein in the mine of developmental techniques.

# Research Resources

"I don't know, Ma'am, why they make all this fuss about education; none of the Pagets can read or write, and they get on well enough."
—WILLIAM LAMB, *Viscount Melbourne*

The University of the Andes and the Center for Studies on Economic Development were the organizations in which I worked for two years. This chapter is devoted to describing them briefly. The University is an important educational institution in Colombia and, indeed, in Latin America. As such, it warrants this attention. Consideration of the early development of CEDE is worthwhile as there are conclusions from the experience which are generally applicable to technical assistance projects.

## THE UNIVERSITY OF THE ANDES

High on the slopes of Guadalupe, the University overlooks downtown Bogotá. The stores, banks, and government offices are only ten minutes walk away—somewhat longer coming back up—yet the campus is a small jewel of tranquility literally walled off from the hustle and bustle of the big capital city. This tranquility, the charm of colonial architecture—not studied, but real,—the beauty of the site somehow make it seem just right for a university. From the office, great stretches of the *savanna*, visible beyond the city, reach for the hills and mountains, marking the edge of the plain. Above, the dazzling white church of Monserate gazes down paternalistically on the whole city, but more especially on the University, so much closer to it. On clear days the splendor of the snowcapped peaks of the central mountain range stands out on the horizon. A more desirable and auspicious spot could hardly have been selected for a university.

The University was founded in 1948 partly in protest against the tradition of Spanish and Colombian higher education, and partly as a protest against the Conservative regime which permeated the other universities. It has grown from an idea to an established university with nearly a thousand students. It offers degrees in engineering, economics, architecture and fine arts, philosophy, and science. Associated with these degree programs are the departments of English, Mathematics, Spanish, Humanities, etc. One innovation will be immediately apparent to those familiar with Latin American universities —the absence of schools of law and medicine.

The influence of the University on Colombian education far exceeds in importance that indicated by the relatively small number of students. As a young and flexible institution with an experimental philosophy it has pioneered in several educational innovations, some of which are now being adopted by other institutions. Some of these merit recounting here.

The University early recognized its own limitations and decided it would be unable to provide high quality education in several curricula. A "three-two" program was developed in several fields. The present engineering course is an example. The engineering student spends his first three university years in Bogotá studying the standard courses for an engineering degree. He also attains oral proficiency in English. After this, he enters a U.S. engineering school as a junior and after two years is awarded a degree by both institutions. If necessary, the University assists the student in financing these two years. Clearly the student receives better training than can be offered in Colombia under present circumstances, and the institution avoids the financial struggle of trying to provide even the minimum and expensive laboratory equipment required for the advanced undergraduate engineering training.

The tendency toward self-sufficiency and vertical isolation was noted as a characteristic of Colombian universities in Chapter VI. In this respect, the University of the Andes much more resembles a gringo university than a Colombian one. "Service departments" in English, Humanities, and Mathematics have been established to avoid the expensive duplication involved in having each faculty provide these courses for itself. The University also recognizes its responsibility to provide more than just professional training for its students. A "general education" program for all students was adopted which now modestly includes Spanish, English, and the Humanities. This is an important improvement in Colombian higher education, and consideration was being given to expanding the "core" of common courses.

The establishment of a research center in economics is another innovation now being emulated by at least one other Colombian university.

A non-degree, two-year premedical program was developed in cooperation with the University of Valle in Cali. This permits Bogotanos to take a part of their training at home before finishing it in what is probably the finest medical school in Colombia. Only flexibility and a certain sense of humility could ever have permitted the establishment of this program.

There is nothing in the above which is at all startling to the U.S. observer who knows only U.S. universities. But these are truly remarkable in Colombian education, and it is even more remarkable that they are all found in a single institution.

The most distinguishing feature of the University of the Andes is that it is a "private" institution. A Latin American university associated with neither the Church nor the State is indeed a rarity. State supported education in the United States is well developed and most of the abuses associated with it have been minimized or eliminated. While church sponsored colleges and universities are important in the United States, they represent many denominations and in no sense can they be considered as appendages of the only or the official religion of the nation. They are just this in Colombia and in most Latin American countries. This dependence of higher education on the State and on the Church has had numerous serious consequences.

State universities have suffered from nearly all the faults of their parent governments. University administrations have frequently been politicaly appointed. Political changes in the administration affect even the lowest professor as he has no civil service, much less a "tenure" concept to protect his job. Nor is the concept of academic freedom well developed, and a professor with unpopular views, from the government's standpoint, may find himself quickly relieved of his duties and salary. In the very best of circumstances, these characteristics may make little difference, but too often they have resulted in bad education and, at worst, universities have become the political tools of incumbent governments rather than being the centers of learning and truthseeking as we idealize them. Perhaps the unrest so typical of Latin American students is in part caused by their lack of respect for the university system—a system which frequently does little to commend it.

It is more difficult to be critical of religiously oriented universities. At the outset, one runs the danger of over-generalizing because there are wide variations in the Roman Catholic Church from country to country and from epoch to epoch. In addition, nearly all the extremes of thought on socio-economic issues are simultaneously held by some of its officials. There is a fine line, too, between honest criticism and bigotry. There are three general areas of potential weakness in church-directed university education although the applicability of these to any given situation depends upon the general status of the Church in its national environment, the degree of control of the university exercised by the Church, and the personalities and philosophies of those charged with the administration of the university.

There are theological limits beyond which solutions to certain problems cannot be sought. In the context of this volume, the "population explosion" is a pressing problem, and the Catholic belief in the inappropriateness of birth control by "artificial" means is clearly related to the issue. For those not of this belief, birth control immediately suggests itself as a topic worthy of consideration, study, and experimentation in a search for means to alleviate the population pressures.[1]

The Catholic Church in Colombia is a far different organization than it is in the United States. As a social institution, it more nearly unifies Colombians than any other organization. It is certainly much stronger than either political party and most likely commands more respect and loyalty than any past government. As a social organism of such importance, it is inevitably political, be this its choice or no. Its utterances, pro or con, public or private, and even its silences have their significances. And its leaders are persons of considerable influence, influence which cannot be restricted to matters spiritual even if the prelates themselves will it. The Church is also an economic organization. In some countries, it has been a major land owner and has fought land reform. In most Latin American countries, it has been a major investor of savings to build church structures which frequently dominate all surrounding buildings.[2] In Colombia, one of the two large labor federations received its organizational impetus from the Church and is still said to be receiving financial support. As a political and economic organization, the Church has interests other than those purely spiritual. In some cases, it has a strong interest in maintaining the *status quo,* and in many cases, it has acted vigorously to do so. That is, there is a strong bias in the Church toward social conservatism. This may or may not be desirable, but in this day of extreme pressures on the *status quo* and great questioning of traditional values and traditional procedures, a university ought to be free and independent in terms of its questioning and investigation. To the extent that the Church does control its educational institutions, this bias may be transmitted to them.

There is considerable opinion that Catholicism provides an environment less conducive to economic growth than that related to some other religious doctrines. To the extent that this is true and to the extent that the fundamental philosophies permeate *the university class-room,* this is unfortunate.[3]

These observations are not intended to be a recommendation for the abolition of public and church-sponsored higher education in Colombia or in Latin America. Rather, they demonstrate the importance of the private institution and specifically emphasize the importance of the University of the Andes in the Colombian environment. There is a great scarcity of higher education regardless of its financial sponsors, but the relative scarcity is greatest in private, independent universities.

The University of the Andes, on the other hand, should not be idealized. It is far from perfect, and a more accurate appraisal can be obtained by looking briefly at some of its short-comings. The most serious is its precarious financing which threatens its greatest strength, its independence. Other than ordinary income from fees, etc., it depends upon annual donations from business. Presently it has no endowment, and the annual fund-raising will become more burdensome to Colombian enterprises with the passage of time or should there be economic difficulties. There has yet been no problem of donor control of the academic program, but such a possibility always is on the horizon and may some time be significant. The University is a leader in employing full-time faculty, but still has far to go to reach standards which most educators would consider acceptable. Of the full-time people, many are paid much too little. The University has been able to trade on their dedication to education. The "idea" of the University has also had enormous appeal to the faculty. But neither are long-run substitutes for adequate salaries. It has the same high rate of student attrition that plagues all Colombian universities and has been able to do nothing about this. Most important are the students dropped in the first year who could finish their university program if some method of making up their initial deficiencies could be found. Such a program is currently being considered. This attrition also results in uneconomically small classes in the final years. The Andes, too, has been plagued with changing administrations. It had five rectors in its first ten years of operation. But a continuing small cadre of persons in key positions has minimized the damage from these frequent changes.

With all its faults, the University of the Andes has a spirit of innovation and of service which captures one as few institutions do.

### CENTER FOR STUDIES ON ECONOMIC DEVELOPMENT

When we arrived in Bogotá in September, 1958, no one had much of an idea of what the Center might become, what it ought to do, or even what might be possible.⁴ The University had a grant to cover my travel expenses and salary and a commitment to match this for two years. Beyond this, it had designated a part-time, part-time (repetition intentional) assistant director and a young man to serve as a personal assistant to me. This, two desks and a chair, were the Center.

*Basic Decisions.* The first few months were spent in seeking personnel, learning as much as possible about Colombia through reading and travel, and in reaching some fundamental decisions regarding CEDE.

It was made explicit that CEDE should have a long life and that planning should envisage it as a viable and Colombian organization. Pragmatically, support from the foundations could not be expected indefinitely. We also felt that after an initial period to get started, CEDE ought to prove itself worthy of continued Colombian support. If it could not do so, the value of continued allocation of resources to it would be doubtful.

We decided only to work in "economic" research as opposed to "business" research. There were elements of pragmatism and principle in this decision as well. Several commercial firms were already engaged in research of a commercial nature and for business interests, and it was agreed that CEDE should neither compete with them nor duplicate their facilities. More important, little effort was being given to "social" research, and we decided that all our efforts ought to be devoted to this end. The research itself was to be useful, and we hoped to demonstrate the general value of this activity to the society.

A fine distinction between "business" and "economic" research is difficult to make. As a rough guide, we interpreted "business" research as being designed primarily to improve the profit and loss position of a particular firm. "Economic" research, on the other hand, was primarily to be concerned with the profit and loss position of society. This distinction is ambiguous in certain areas, but it allowed us to make clear decisions in most cases and also proved to be an acceptable means of explaining CEDE's objectives.

It immediately became evident that financial planning was necessary. The first two years were not crucial because of the Rockefeller Foundation grant and the University's matching commitment. But it was likewise clear that CEDE could not expect or justify support of this magnitude from the University over long periods. Resources were too limited and the needs of the instructional program too great. Thus we accepted the principle that CEDE would have to earn much of its way through contract research. Although there are disadvantages to this type of research, it has the obvious advantage of producing income and the less obvious one of testing one's wares and reputation in the market place.

As the shortage of trained and competent personnel became alarmingly apparent, it also became clear that CEDE would have to undertake a long-range and continuing training program. And for similar reasons, it became a part of our task to develop an adequate research library.

*Basic Problems.* Recruiting personnel was by far the most serious problem of the Centro. There simply exists no pool of well-trained persons waiting to accept this sort of position. There is not, for example, one Colombian with a Ph.D. in economics.[5] Those with graduate training were already in responsible positions in the government or in well-paying jobs in industry. In the case of the former, it seemed not desirable to try to hire them away from these positions; in the case of the latter, it would have been foolish to try. Thus, it became necessary for the Centro to develop its own personnel.

Largely by accident, a satisfactory recruiting program was developed. The initial "staff" of CEDE was three young men who had finished their course work in the University of the Andes but who had not yet finished their thesis requirements. They were hired for a four-month period with nominal salaries and given the title of "assistant." They selected research tasks of interest to themselves and to the Center and which were also acceptable to the faculty as theses. During their period of employment as assistants, they were regarded as regular staff members and received the support normally accorded such persons— travel expenses, secretarial assistance, and supervision. All three worked out well, and when their degree requirements were finally completed, they joined the staff as regular and permanent staff members at substantial increases in salary. This procedure worked so well that it was adopted as a regular part of the program of the Center and budgetary arrangements were made to carry at least three assistants throughout the year. The program was also expanded to include such persons from other universities. This scheme was the major source of personnel for the two-year period, although other persons were added from time to time.

All staff members had at least some research experience when they became permanent staff members (some through the assistant route), but experience was very scanty and none had more formal training than the B.A. degree or its Colombian equivalent. Thus, there was a considerable need to increase the qualifications of the staff, and this was undertaken in several ways: (1) The least formal, but most important, method was the close day-to-day participation of the director in project development and supervision. Frequent staff meetings were held to discuss problems and progress, and these contributed substantially to our knowledge of project design, research techniques, editing. (2) Later, a series of seminars was initiated with speakers from outside the University who were engaged in economic research of one sort or another. (3) A long-run staff development plan was also initiated which consists largely of securing graduate training abroad for staff members. Through the foundations, the Department of State, and other means, one staff member has earned his doctorate and returned. Another has completed his M.A. program. Three others were taking graduate courses in various U.S. institutions in academic year 1961-62. These opportunities were developed by CEDE, and the recipients agree to return to the Center after completing their training. Further, and most important, sufficiently attractive salary schedules have been arranged so that they can comfortably return to CEDE.

Salaries were not generally an important recruiting device although an agreement was finally reached with the University that permitted offering salaries that were at least "mildly competitive" with existing alternatives. This was an extremely important "break-through" when one recalls the traditional approach of Colombian universities to faculty salaries. Most attractive to prospective staff members was the seriousness of the research being conducted, the congeniality of the group, freedom from the usual harassments associated with working in governmental offices, and the possibilities of heavily subsidized training abroad. In addition, personal prestige was an attraction because much of our work involved contacts with important Colombians. Thus, staff members had the opportunity to become known personally and to attract attention through frequent publication.

The basic financial arrangements included the grant from the Rockefeller Foundation and a matching commitment by the University for other expenditures. This basic foundation grant was subsequently renewed for another two years beginning August, 1960. Supplemental grants for statistical equipment and library purchases were also made. The University more than met its commitment during the first two years. It was generally recognized that these were two crucial years and that considerable resources should be devoted to insuring a good start by the Center. Both the administration and I felt, however, that the sums required (in the neighborhood of $25,000 U.S. per year) were far more than the University could justify over any long period.

As already noted, it was decided early that much of the support of the Center would have to come from its own income earned in doing contract research. A budget agreement was reached with the University which permitted sharing equally the benefits of the contract income between the University's budgetary liability and CEDE. This involved the concept of a maximum-minimum budget. The minimum contribution of the University was to cover certain administrative expenses and library acquisitions regardless of the amount of contract income. The maximum amount was to provide for a minimum staff should no contract income be forthcoming. Between these two extremes, contract income was to be divided equally between reducing the University's liability for financing the Center and increasing the Center's operating budget. This at once provided for reducing the too-large drain on University resources and for expansion of CEDE.

Even in the second year, substantial contract income was earned, and since then contracts for even greater amounts have been negotiated. This long-run budgetary pressure affected somewhat the type of research undertaken. We tended to undertake projects which would produce publishable results in a relatively short period of time because long-range, group research would have tied up most of the staff for long periods with no publicly apparent results. The necessity of establishing a reputation was responsible for this bias.

In the two-year period an acceptable quantity of research was completed and published. Quality suffered (as compared to U.S. standards) both because of relatively inexperienced personnel and much more difficult research conditions than would normally be part of the problem in the United States. Costs, however, were lower, so that one might speculate that output per dollar of input was not far different than one would find in the United States. Initially, a "research cata-logue" was established which included projects of interest to members of the staff which seemed desirable and within our expected means. This led immediately to a search to discover what had already been done on these subjects so that any efforts on our part would not duplicate something already done. Bibliographic aids were found to be extremely poor, so the first major project undertaken was the preparation and publication of a bibliography on economic development and the Colombian economy. This annotated bibliography, containing some 1,700 items, was published and a second volume produced in 1961.

Criteria in determining research undertakings were, at best, not well defined. Contract research objectives, of course, were determined by negotiating with the "customer." For the assistants, projects were selected which were possible in the short period of time available to them. Some useful and otherwise desirable projects were discarded because basic data were not available. Other than these, project selection was made on the basis of the importance of the project, the capabilities and interest of staff members, and the probabilities of finding significant and useful results. For public relations reasons, other things being equal, a short project was preferred to a long one.

In terms of problems encountered in doing research, the nature of the existing data has been noted in previous chapters. In some cases, we found that data had been collected but was "reserved" by government offices and could not be made available to us. In the absence of plentiful data, we found ourselves employing statistical methods which would shock researchers in the United States. One project, for example, would have required all the budget available to establish a statistically acceptable sample, and in this case we had to decide that the sample would have to be less than perfect so that some time and effort could be devoted to seeking results. Another study produced results not conforming to those desired by the contractor, and he threatened to withhold payment until more palatable results could be "found." This problem was left in the hands of my successor, who ultimately resolved it without compromise, but with threatened legal action.

*Conclusions.* I was well pleased with the progress we made in the two years in Bogotá. In view of the negative impressions left by such works as *The Ugly American* and *Is the World Our Campus?* [6] concerning technical assistance, it is worthwhile to try briefly to isolate those factors which contributed to whatever success we achieved: (1) Most important was the genuine interest and continuous support of the University of the Andes. The idea was initiated by the University and its perseverance finally resulted in a Center. It was deeply committed financially and morally from the beginning. The Rector and Dean of the faculty provided continuous support, encouragement, and assistance as did other officials of the University. (2) Good luck led to the development of a staff, professional and secretarial, which was congenial, loyal, and dedicated to the objectives of the Center. (3) As a foreigner, I was probably able to accomplish more than an equally well qualified Colombian might have, at least in broaching such traditions as low salaries, etc. It does not follow that if one gringo is good, however, that five would be five times as good. In spite of its foreign leadership, CEDE was generally considered to be a Colombian institution. (4) It was pleasant to be free of responsibility to any government. The fact that I had no official association with the U.S. government made my acceptance in Colombian circles much easier. (5) The youth and consequent flexibility of the University of the Andes made the innovations required possible; they would have been much more difficult in more tradition-centered institutions. (6) The continued interest and help of the foundations especially in providing scholarship aid to staff members for study abroad will prove to have been a critical contribution in the years to come. (7) Originally, my commitment was for only one year. Two years proved to be an absolute minimum; one year would have hardly been worth the effort for myself or for the University.

# Green Fever

"Green fever is a contagious disease, spread by contact, particularly endemic in Colombia. Foreign travelers are particularly susceptible. Symptomatology is equivocal with particularly great variations in severity. The disease is often progressive. Sleeplessness is a common complaint. Eyes frequently becomes fixed and glassy, or may show rapid alternations in gaze between objects. Tremor of the hand or fingers, especially the fourth digit, may be noted . . . Treatment is palliative. Chemotherapy and antibiotics are ineffectual. Relapses are frequent and may occur at regular or irregular intervals. Long term survival rate is usually not affected. Therapy consists of the judicious use of rich green beryl in the crystalline form in adequate dosage."

—JESSIE WADDELL

An emerald is a bit of beryl crystal that got mixed up with enough chromic oxide in its growth process to give it a velvety rich green brilliance. Emeralds, less hard than diamonds, are used only for ornament.[1] Little is known about the geology of their formation, but it is well known that a gem-sized stone with fire and clarity and a deep green color is equal in value to a good diamond of comparable size. And it is known that since the days of the conquistadors that most of the world's fine emeralds have come from the mountains of Colombia. This knowledge is enough to produce a fever in the hearts of more than a few in and near Bogotá. Intimacy with the emerald business provided us off-the-beaten-track experience and more than enough of the seamy side of human nature.

Emerald production is not an important aspect of the Colombian economy and perhaps never was. In 1957, mining as an industry only contributed 3.1 per cent of the national income, and in 1958, only 1.4 per cent of the labor force was employed in mining.[2] Emerald production is only a small part of Colombian mining, and it is doubtful if more than 400 persons are actively engaged in it. These stones were not even of sufficient importance to record them in the exports of 1958 although a substantial value was surely exported through non-commercial channels.[3]

Emeralds were well known to the pre-Columbian civilizations, and their presence as far north as Mexico and as far south as Inca Peru is one of the few clues to the interrelations of these early Americans. In a brief, serious account, Michael Weinstein records an emerald "as broad as the palm of the hand" in a shipment of loot from Cortes to the Emperor of Spain in 1525. Cortes later carried five magnificent stones with him to Spain, and his refusal to part with them led to royal displeasure and contributed to his banishment from the court. The conquistadors of the south under Pizarro were less astute than their northern counterparts in the matter of emeralds. The landing in 1531 "resulted in the capture of an enormous quantity of precious stones, as well as a large number of valuable gold and silver ornaments. Of the stones, emeralds were the most abundant, and one, which fell into the hands of Pizarro, was as large as a pigeon's egg. Unfortunately, his followers did not understand the value of such gems, and they broke many into fragments by pounding them with hammers. It is recorded that they were encouraged in this destruction by one of the accompanying missionaries, Fray Reginaldo de Pedraza, who assured them that this was the right method of testing a real emerald. He asserted that true stones would not be affected by such treatment. But it was observed that the good father did not subject his own jewels to this test." [4]

It is difficult, at best, to analyze the mining of emeralds in the usual type of industrial analysis applied by economists. In the first place, the "product" is far from homogeneous. Each stone is like no other. The value of a stone depends partly upon its size, and value varies more or less geometrically with size. Almost all emeralds have imperfections ("gardens"), and value also depends upon the relative absence of these imperfections. Color is another important consideration with the deep green stones receiving preference.[5] Finally, stones vary in lustre, brilliance, or "fire."

Marketing is highly disorganized because of the relatively small production of recent years and because much of the trade has been illicitly conducted. Varying degrees of control are exercised by the government from outright ownership of mining properties to taxation of output. One outfit allegedly conducted a broad daylight holdup of its own courier to avoid evaluation of its output by the government and subsequent taxation. (A government inspector at the mine would possibly have reported the shipment). Not much can be said of the foreign demand for these gems, although over relevant ranges, price elasticity probably is very high. That is, output could probably be doubled or tripled without seriously affecting prices in New York or Europe although prices in Bogotá vary considerably with output.

Further, there seems to be very little relation between domestic Colombian prices and prices abroad. We know of one case where a set ring, costing about $300 in Bogotá was appraised at over $1500 in the United States. Even the 45 per cent duty on set stones and high jewelers' mark-ups, hardly accounts for such a difference.

Even less can be said with confidence about the cost or "supply" side of the industry. As little is known about the geology of the emerald, prospecting presents the first problem, and the costs of this are incalculable. Deposits are highly localized in small pockets not necessarily within easily identified masses. Prospecting and seeking mining concessions must be carried on simultaneously because the fever runs high when the countryside learns that emerald prospecting is going on—tempers flare and the race to the Ministry of Mines is on when serious prospectors appear. As one might imagine, there are certain costs which can hardly appear on the books in connection with securing a concession.

Once governmental approval is obtained, mining can begin. Before anything else can be done, security must be provided—a safe set in concrete, weapons permits, police protection. What fisherman would go out without a landing net or gaff? Completing the nimrod analogy, the least accessible spots seem to be preferred for prospecting.

The operation is hardly "mining" at all. It must be done by hand because blasting or mechanical crushing would destroy the precious crystals. Small groups of men, closely supervised, hack out terraces in the "most likely spots" (picked largely by the boss' intuition). When things look "promising," this work is literally done by hand. Costs per day are low as labor is cheap, food is cheap, and only a few workers can be well supervised. Tools cost next to nothing.

Most mining is carried on where emeralds are known to have been found in the past. This puts great emphasis on searching out historical accounts, even to those of the conquistadors, and a well executed "treasure map" could be disposed of like hotcakes. This traditional approach was rudely upset and all the fevers started anew only a few years ago when a strike was made in a new area. No one outside the firm knows what the output at this site has been, but rumor has it in this industry that lives on rumor that the "gross" has been one to five million dollars. Of this, 80-90 per cent must have been "net."

Such an industry defies neat analysis in terms of sweeping curves of average and marignal costs. And it defies more sophisticated analysis of probabilities, etc. It requires personal courage, tremendous perseverance, an unholy optimism, willingness to "play" rough without much regard to morality. Other than this a little capital is required each year plus all the luck in the world.

\*　　\*　　\*

With this as background, these are personal experiences with "green fever." I recount it for three reasons. First of all, it is worth the telling as a story. Beyond this, it may help explain something of the appeal of overseas assignments to the stodgy, ivory-towered professor. Finally, in true professorial tradition, there is something of a moral to the ending of my part of the story.

More or less by accident, we became acquainted with an ex- and would-be emerald miner. At the time, he was destitute and ekeing out an existence supplying emeralds and other stones to the foreign community in Bogotá on a commission basis. We will call him Mr. M. He was lonely, good to us and to the kids, and we soon became good friends. Not long after this friendship began to develop, Mr. M. made connections with a U.S. firm that was interested in undertaking emerald mining operations, and a second character in the drama appeared who shall be known as Mr. X. He came to Colombia to become acquainted with Mr. M. and to look over possible concessions. This was during the time that I was devoting a good deal of effort to becoming acquainted with Colombia, and when these two invited me to accompany them on two of their trips, I eagerly accepted.

The first of these trips was to the government-owned and Bank of the Republic operated mines at Muzo. From these mines have come the finest emeralds in the world; they are especially notable for their deep color. This proved to be a delightful trip, first by a one-car train for about three hours and then down, down, down off the savanna to the mine site by rented car. During this particular season, the flame trees were in full bloom and the mountainsides we descended were tinged with red from the profusion of these beautiful trees.

The beauty of this spot cannot be adequately described—set on the banks of a low tropical gorge with flame trees in full bloom and mists clinging to the verdant mountainsides—so far removed from the turbulence of Bogotá and the toils and troubles of the rest of the world. This physical setting, though, provides only an illusion of peace when one recalls the violent and turbulent history of mining in this very location. We were permitted to inspect the terraces where mining had been carried on, but every move was in the presence of an armed guard. *He* found a couple of small crystals.

Little was being done in the way of mining operations. My impression, perhaps erroneous, was that mining operations were being avoided as much as possible. Men were erecting buildings and the construction of a road to Coscuez, another promising mining site some 8-10 hours away by horse, was being planned. The administrator seemed determined to have something to show for the expenditure of his budget and roads and buildings seemed sufficient. But if he spent money for mining operations and failed to produce emeralds, then nothing would have been accomplished, and he probably would have lost his job. Such a hypothesis is difficult to verify but it is not atypical of bureaucracy and represents an understandable reaction to the uncertainties of this business.

The "mines" are nothing more than two terraced mountainsides, one on either side of the valley. The rich, carbon-black earth contains veins of snow-white calcite, and at Muzo, it is in these veins that emeralds are found—when they are found at all. Only the surface has been scratched over the centuries, and no one can know what may be included in the bowels of these mountains. The camaraderie that developed among the three of us added greatly to the pleasure of this very instructive trip.

A week or so later the three of us set off again, this time to inspect the area Mr. M. specifically planned to work. This involved a trip to the northeast of Bogotá, some six hours by jeep. We stayed all night in the village of Gachalá (to which we return later) and the following day took off by horse and mule through very rugged and fantastic scenery to inspect the property. It was near Gachalá that the new strike was made a few years ago, and Mr. M's proposed concession abutted this operation. Mr. X and I rode an additional hour or two to visit the Gachalá mine only to be driven off at the point of a gun. Mr. M, being a *persona non grata* with these operators, did not even approach the place. Again, the trip was pleasant, informative, and friendly—although at the end of our eight hour ride, no one was too comfortable and something more than a Colombian village hotel with board beds (and bugs) would have been appealing.

I never saw or heard from Mr. X again, although we parted on the best of terms and he returned to Bogotá several times. The result of this first visit was an agreement between the group he represented and Mr. M to undertake a mining operation. Mr. X was to bring to the agreement a relatively small amount of capital and Mr. M was to bring his concessions, know-how, and the willingness to live at the end of the world to conduct the operations. This was the high point of the agreement, and from here it went down hill. There were delays in getting the concessions finally approved because of a new mining law proposed by the Ministry of Mines. Attendant with these delays, there were stories of all sorts of chicanery in the Ministry of Mines with tales of "lost" papers, missed deadlines, improper surveys, etc.— all evidence of the fair and unfair competition for what was thought to be a desirable concession.

During this time, Mr. M moved a small crew to Batatas, a village of three houses about two and a half hours by horse from Gachalá and about an hour from the proposed mine. We made a family visit there for what we expected to be a couple of days. Due to prolonged rain, however, it was impossible to return for some eight days—eight days of board beds and the most vicious bug we have ever encountered, the *jejene*. Parenthetically, these rains washed out a bridge between Gachalá and Bogotá and although we were able to get back to Bogotá by bus, the jeep stayed there for an additional six weeks. For several weeks, this whole section of the country had to be serviced by hand-carrying goods across the river on an improvised bridge.

On two other occasions, we visited Mr. M in the field. Both of these times were in Guateque, just across the valley from the Somondoco mine properties, so often mentioned in emerald literature. Somondoco is not far as the crow flies, but further as the mule plods, from the still-worked Chivor mines. Muzo is hours and a couple of hundred miles away. On one of these occasions a family, on a Fulbright fellowship in Bogotá, accompanied us.

We never learned all the details of the breakup of the partnership between Mr. M and Mr. X and his group. We heard only one side of the story and did not believe all that we heard. We suspected that the incurable optimism of Mr. M was rationalizing a failure to produce. He alleged that Mr. X was trying to squeeze him out completely and gain the concessions entirely for himself since they were listed in the name of the agreeing parties. We heard tales of bribing Colombian officials to have Mr. M declared a *persona non grata* and ejected from the country. To all this we loaned a sympathetic but somewhat non-believing ear, thinking such behavior impossible from a person such as Mr. X and also discounting much of this as coming from a highly biased source.

Only later did we inadvertently learn something of the truth. The necessity of renewing our passports took us to the U.S. embassy, and in the process of getting this done, one of the consular officers took us aside and queried us in mysterious fashion about our relations with

Mr. M. After a few questions, we declined to answer further without information as to why we were being queried. We were then told that Mr. X had indeed written the Secretary of State of the United States, Senator Fulbright, and to the U.S. Ambassador to Colombia urging that Mr. M be declared a *persona non grata* in Colombia on the grounds that he was dishonest, incompetent, immoral (with specifics), etc. This was incredible behavior from our knowledge of Mr. X, but even more startling was learning that our association with Mr. M was described in some detail, including the details of our visits with him in the field and our hospitality to him in Bogotá. Embassy officials and the "Fulbright family" were also included. The implication was that our association made us some sort of correspondent in all the charged corruption, including sexual deviation. The end sought was to discourage the Embassy from renewing the passport of such an "evil influence" who had so obviously corrupted all these fine people. I asked to see the letter, but the request was denied. There is no doubt of its existence.

For us, this was a big adventure. It contributed spice and romance to our living in Bogotá and gave us an opportunity to observe mankind in the raw—seeking great wealth. It was valuable to us both as recreation and education, but there is a lingering worry. What has happened to the copies of the letter? Security clearance may be important to me at any time. Have these allegations, if they are worthy of the name, been added to my *dossier* somewhere? The next time clearance becomes necessary, will these comments require investigation? The fact that we do worry, not about the substance, but about the possibility that such nonsense may have been filed is a serious commentary upon the legacy of McCarthy which still lingers.

## IX

# American Viewpoint

"Jonas acquired some reputation by travelling abroad, but lost it all
by travelling at home."

—Boswell's *Life of Johnson*

Professors Walter Adams and John A. Garraty recently produced a
provocative little book, *Is the World our Campus?*[1] as the result of an
intensive study of the effectiveness of university contracts (and hence
"professors") abroad. Their study was largely confined to Europe
which in part predetermines their conclusions.

In one chapter, "The American Expert Abroad," they are highly
critical of both the quality of persons on these missions and their behavior both as representatives of the United States and of their universities. One infers this from their discussion and the positioning of
their comments rather than from any clear unequivocal conclusions.
They do not insist that all overseas professors are bad and do cite
examples of good appointments. But the intent is clearly negative
criticism. The chapter concludes as follows:

"The basic difficulty, some foreign observers believe, is that too
many 'technical assistance experts' go overseas, not to help others but
to raise their own standard of living. And this cannot be stated too
often.

"Once he goes abroad under an ICA-university contract, the professor's way of life changes radically. His salary is increased from a nine-
month to a twelve-month basis, and supplemented by a 'hardship differ-
ential' depending on the area to which he is assigned. He gets a 'post'
allowance and, unless housing is provided, a housing allowance as well.
If he stays abroad for more than 18 months, his pay is exempt from U.S.
income tax. Unless he lives on an utterly reckless scale, he can save
anywhere from $5,000 to $10,000 while abroad. Not only does he have
more dollars to spend, but each dollar buys more than at home. Probably for the first time in his life, the professor can afford the luxury of
servants and his wife can escape the routine drudgery of household
chores. Finally, he can join the diplomatic cocktail circuit and move
up [sic] socially. The professor, partly because his academic rank is
a badge of prestige and partly because he is regarded as a representa-

tive of the United States, acquires new status. He rubs shoulders with foreign dignitaries and 'inspection-touring' American Congressmen. Gradually the professor acquires a sense of importance, a feeling that he too is a V.I.P." [2]

I have no notion of undertaking a global defense of my far-flung colleagues. In the first place, my observations are limited to two situations. And in the second place, I have seen too many recruiting mistakes not to recognize that there have been some rotten ones in the overseas apple barrel. On the other hand, I have seen little evidence to indicate that universities have done a poorer job of recruiting than other agencies who dispatch people overseas—including ICA itself. [3] I will not soon forget the shocking performance of one senior ICA official who, on his first meeting with the Governor of the central bank of Viet Nam, shook his finger in the Governor's face and said, "There'll be no inflation in this country while *I* am here." [4]

It should be made clear, too, that the Adams and Garraty "campus" has been severely circumscribed by dealing only with ICA-contract professors. Academicians are working abroad under many circumstances and with varying financial rewards, some of which require substantial personal monetary sacrifices. Some work directly with the U.S. government, some are on private contracts with international organizations or with foreign institutions, some are employed by the foundations, and some work and live inelegantly under Fulbright or Smith-Mund grants. ICA-contract personnel are treated more liberally than most, and the Adams-Garraty indictment can be applied, if at all, only partially to non-ICA professors.

The quotation above over-exaggerates the matter of finances, although it is difficult to generalize for all countries for all times. The professorial salary is put on an annual basis by converting it from a nine-months to a twelve-months base. The "duty" time is proportionately increased as well, and as Adams and Garraty know, most professors have at least the occasional option of teaching in summer school or accepting some other summer assignment for purposes of supplementing their incomes. This is not infrequent behavior in the year when a new car must be bought or a new room added or an illness paid for. In other words, this income opportunity is generally available to the professor at home and the annualization gives him no additional income. "Hardship," "post," and "housing" allowances vary considerably from country to country, and presumably their justification varies considerably as well. [5]

The professor under this kind of contract may have more dollars, but it is not always true that "each dollar buys more than at home." This, too, varies from country to country. One can argue pedantically that the purchasable items available differ so greatly that it is not possible to compare costs of living between countries, but this does not come to grips with the Adams-Garraty point. We estimated that the cost of living in Bogotá was, at best, slightly higher than in the U.S. A few items illustrate the basis of our estimation. Housing was expensive, and a smaller house there cost $75 per month more than we received for our stateside house. On arrival in Bogotá, I bought a four-year old jeep for about $1,600 U.S. and in the next two years spent approximately $500 U.S. on it in major repairs. Meat and some other foodstuffs were cheap, but many were expensive. Eggs, butter,[6] and an occasional fowl were hard on the family budget. On balance, we figured living in Colombia cost us a bit more.

It is sometimes argued that gringos abroad should not try to live like gringos but rather should live as do their hosts. This is reasonable and necessary in certain circumstances, i.e., when working in the field with host-country personnel, but as a general rule it is impractical to "when in Colombia, do as the Colombians do." It is nonsense both from the point of view of one's psychological well-being and his health. Had we eaten a Colombian diet, our food costs would have been substantially lower and it would have been two years of a culinary hell—all starch. The presence of children also makes this impractical. There are enough adjustments to be made without undertaking unnecessary, unpalatable ones. Nor does this mean that one should insist on eating, for example, exactly as he does at home. This is too expensive, if possible at all, and also eliminates many exciting gastatory experiences—to say nothing of embarrassment when invited out. Generally, this has meant for us considerable use of the more expensive foods available in the local markets—frequently provided specifically for the gringos. Infrequent use of expensive potatoes as a substitute for twice daily rice, for example, was an extremely welcome change in Viet Nam.

The Adams-Garraty indictment does not directly include the "palatial living" criticism raised by others. Gringo professors sometimes do live in "palaces" and perhaps more frequently than they should.[7] But this is by no means universal. In three of four of our "overseas" houses, we have had fewer rooms or less space than in our modest modified Michigan Cape Cod. In Bogotá, our last house fell something short of the "palace" classification, but it was large— and at our personal expense as well.

Adams and Garraty seem to be bothered by servants in professor's homes[8] and this is taken as clear evidence that we never had it so good. Again, partly true, but far short of the whole picture.  Consider the extreme example of the Hunter experience:  Viet Nam, where we had five (!) servants.  (No one can ever say that I haven't met a payroll!) This, for a two bedroom house, ought to have been heaven by anyone's standards.

For the most part, however, these very lovely people substituted for capital equipment common in the U.S. home.  The combination of climate and a very small refrigerator made it necessary that the food shopping be done daily— maybe two miles away by *ciclopousse* in a market whose stench was amazing and bargaining required.  One of our entourage did most of the shopping each day and did the cooking on gas or on charcoal.  Cooking included boiling the large amounts of water consumed daily by the household and trying to beat powdered milk into something like a palatable liquid.  The climate required constant changes of clothing for all five, and the twins were still in diapers.  Another of the menage substituted for the washing machine and drier—doing laundry for hours daily on a cement slab and endless amounts of ironing.

Two *amahs* were a bit of luxury.  We hired the "assistant" nurse-maid when the first had a baby of her own, and *we* thought it desirable that she be free to spend at least a part of each day with her own child.  Again, the nursemaids had tasks greater than conventional "baby-sitters" in the U.S. "Security" required that the one child be taken every day to school and met when school was out.  There was no playing alone outside the fence surrounding the house, and someone had to be with the kids each minute they were in the park.  Thus, the *amahs* did make life easier than it is in the United States, but doing without them would have imposed parental burdens not found state-side.  The function of the fifth servant was somewhat ambiguous— she was coordinator for all, served as vacuum cleaner and carpet sweeper, dishwasher, etc.

This is not at all to deny that life was easier and more pleasant. Clearly, my wife had more time to be a person and to do things which she could not otherwise have done. But the point is that servants abroad to a large extent are necessary to undertake some of the tasks unique to living abroad and to substitute for mechanical appliances which are a customary part of our living in the U.S.  Surely Adams and Garraty would not have us send our wives back to the nineteenth century.

Life in Colombia is less demanding of manual service, but at least one servant per family is required for protection against burglary on occasions of absence. Having servants is not all a bed of roses, however delightful it may seem. Adjusting to living with five Vietnamese or two Colombians, selected haphazardly, is not easy—teaching, supervising, understanding and misunderstanding them. There is a good deal of frustration—probably on both sides of the bargain.[9]

There are some additional risks and expenses which Adams and Garraty do not take into account. I list these without detailed comment. (1) From the time we agreed to go to Bogotá until we got there, school costs nearly doubled. (One might counter this with the argument that taxes might increase similarly in the States. They did, and we paid them, too). (2) There is increased risk of loss from theft. (3) Risk of illness is higher in some areas in spite of the attempt to innoculate against everything before leaving. Paying for a course or two of amoeba cures is not inconsiderable. (4) On two occasions, we had to sell a just-broken-in car before leaving the States. This was expensive. (5) Believe it or not, there are exchange risks. In Bogotà we saw the rate fall from $8.15 pesos per dollar to $6.80. This represented a substantial reduction in income when most expenditures were in pesos. (6) One's mode of living changes, too. As one example, in the States we are accustomed to camping vacations. In both Colombia and Viet Nam, this was impossible; more expensive vacations were necessary—to the extent that we took them. (7) There is a possible tax risk. Only when we left Colombia finally did we *know* that we were not subject to Colombian income tax—which incidentally would have been considerable higher than U.S. levy on the same income. (8) We spent several hundred dollars in two years in Bogotá for language instruction. Some ICA contracts cover this, so language lessons are not a personal expense for all language-deficient professors overseas. (9) It has been our experience that returning to the United States has been expensive. There is always the house to be renovated, appliances to be replaced or repaired, installation charges.

All this discussion of money is not to complain. Persons luckier than we or better managers may have saved the amounts suggested by Adams and Garraty. They may or may not have been worth their salaries. The purpose in looking at this in such detail is to indicate that there is more to the question than a hurried comparison of the overseas gross with the professor's nine-months stateside salary.

Adams and Garraty seem also to deprecate the sense of importance acquired by the overseas professor. "He rubs shoulders with foreign dignitaries and 'inspection-touring' American Congressmen. Gradually, the professor acquires a sense of importance, a feeling that he too is a 'V.I.P.'" [10] He *is* a V.I.P., and the sooner he realizes it the better. He is likely the only one, or one of the very few, in the country with experience and knowledge in his specialty. After living in the country a while, he may very well be the best qualified person to brief the visiting fireman interested in his specialty. He may also serve as a very useful "check" to provide independent opinion from those who are seeking funds or those seeking to justify a program. He *is* there because the country lacks sufficient experts in his specialty, and it may very well be that ministers and other high officials will seek his counsel —and well they might. Rather than criticizing the sense of self-importance, the overseas professor should be told that he is consequential, that he may be asked for opinions regarding questions more critical than he has ever had to deal with before, and above all that someone might even act on his advice. And he should be told, too, that he will not be operating in an environment of colleagues eager to attack him in the journals or forums to point out the weaknesses of his arguments. No, rather than worry that he might develop a sense of importance, we should worry that he might not develop it soon enough. He is important and only when he realizes this will he develop the vital humility and sense of responsibility that must accompany his importance.

To be candid, I admit enjoying some of the contacts with visiting firemen and being in a position to act as a source of information to them. [11] We became intimately acquainted with a number of important gringos we would not have known outside the foreign context. But I do not feel defensive about this nor do I think that I should. These people were in Bogotá because they had some interest in Colombia. I had lived, travelled, and worked there; I was pleased and qualified to share with them whatever I had learned. Nor will I feel defensive about the sense of importance that I developed in Bogotá. I was almost uniquely qualified to do the job I was hired to do; practically no one else in Colombia had the education, the experience, or the willingness to do this particular job. The contribution of the 3,000th economist in the United States may not amount to much and he could disappear without being missed. But the opportunities for the fifth, tenth, or twentieth economist in Colombia to perform important and useful services are enormous. We go because we are scarce in the host countries; because we are scarce, our contributions can be important. Let us keep the sense of importance, please, and let us be humble in the face of it.

❋   ❋   ❋

Adams and Garraty devote considerable attention to describing the characteristics of a "good academic ambassador." [12] Their list of desirable characteristics includes: technical competence, adaptability including that of his family, patience, cultural empathy including the willingness to at least make a pass at learning the local language, and diplomacy. "Humility" sneaks in only through the back door. I have no serious quarrel with this list—in fact, it seems a good list for a person in almost any job here and abroad. The importance of each characteristic varies a great deal with the assignment involved. Patience, diplomacy are not crucial if the task is purely research, while adaptability might be of utmost importance. If the task involves supervision of host nationals, other characteristics assume greater importance.

"Humility" deserves a great deal more emphasis than Adams and Garraty give it. In the first place, it must be realized from the start that one's foreign colleagues will know infinitely more about the society, culture, and institutions of the country than will the foreign professor even though they may be technically less competent and may have less time to devote to pursuit of the objectives of the particular mission. Since we are dealing in change of some sort or another and since change involves people, a knowledge of the economic and social environment is an absolute requirement for most technicians—even those in the physical sciences. The foreign professor unwilling to approach these assignments with a sense of humility about his own ignorance in these affairs and without the patience to undertake acquiring a minimum of such knowledge had better stay home. And he needs his sense of humility when finally he can start proposing and initiating change.

This doesn't mean that the professor abroad need lean forever on his foreign colleagues and depend entirely on their notions of what will work and what will not. They too can be wrong, have vested interests, and may be less experienced. The visiting professor must depend on his colleagues, but at the same time he must develop his own independent knowledge and judgment.

One other aspect of the professor abroad needs a great deal more stress than Adams and Garraty give it. The personal characteristics of the professor's family, especially those of his wife, are of nearly equal importance to the god-like attributes sought in the professor. We have seen several good technicians continually discontent because their wives could not or would not adapt gracefully to living abroad. An unhappy home situation can destroy one's effectiveness at the office. In the worst of situations, we saw wives whose discontent and antagonism were public knowledge and who consequently nullified the good work of their husbands.

A willingness to commit himself for relatively long periods of time is also an important characteristic in selecting an overseas professor. Adams and Garraty cite the case of one Professor Gatenby[13] quietly working by himself in Turkey for ten years and accomplishing much more than that achieved in a short-term, team project employing more than thirty man-years. With the stress given earlier to the importance of immersing oneself in the culture and economy of the host country, this characteristic assumes additional importance. This immersion requires time, travel, reflection, so that only after the first year does the technician begin to become valuable—competent to apply his special knowledge to the environment of the host country. For most tasks, a minimum assignment of two years is essential.

There are corollary implications to this requirement. More time and effort should be spent in recruiting, including when necessary the opportunity for the prospective professor to visit the post in advance. At least this will reduce the "I-didn't-know-it-would-be-like-this-and-I-want-to-leave" cases. The cost seems great, but it would be a small percentage of the total and could result in a substantial improvement in personnel recruited. Programs stand or fall on their overseas staffs.

Finally, some understanding is required between the professor and his university regarding the value the institution places on foreign activity. Research, articles written theses supervised, papers given—usually highly regarded by universities—will be neglected by the overseas professor. The university need not place a high value on his activities, but much discontent can be avoided by a clear understanding on this matter so that the professor may estimate in advance the career effects of his sojourn abroad. Although his activity may ultimately increase his "marketability," he takes himself out of the market for some time.

*       *       *


Two other aspects of the life of the affluent professor overseas are worthy of mention.

One of the more important effects that have come to our notice is the increased importance of the family as a unit. There are generally fewer "routine distractions." In place of television, the kids planned and put on their own shows for their parents. Weekends were frequently devoted to family trips, picnics, going to the races, hiking, and the like—in place of the movies, swimming lessons, house repair, lawn mowing. After dinner we read together and played games as a family while, for a very pleasant change, someone else did the dishes. Fewer meetings intruded into our evenings, and we found time to talk and to reintroduce ourselves to reading for pleasure. Studying languages together has also been a fruitful and enjoyable task.

On the other hand, part of the family self-sufficiency resulted from the necessity to severely restrict the independence of the kids— they could not be permitted to roam the streets even in the immediate neighborhood as they do in the States. Visiting the homes of other children required more planning, and thus occurred less frequently than usually is the case; this was unfortunate. But on balance, we regard this "togetherness" a desirable characteristic of living abroad. But it could make worse a family situation already strained in its stateside environment.

In our collective penchant for self-examination, there is a fertile field of study in the reaction of overseas dependents to their experiences, for clearly it is on these that the greatest changes are wrought. The professor has his work which varies only in degree from his familiar tasks at home, and perhaps he finds it even more rewarding and fascinating.

The change for the wife is the greatest. She can, and generally does, have more leisure. She has a household to run with servants instead of machines, and the problem of communication may be even more difficult with the former. She has to make do with what she can find on local markets to meet the culinary tastes of her demanding children and perhaps finicky husband. As the major purchaser for the family, she has to enter the world of bargaining which may be distasteful. She hears constantly the exact state of health of her friends and their friends and friends of theirs (a more popular topic than kids), and she has good reason to worry about the health of her family. The constant threat of burglary may impose a strain and, depending on the country, fears of civil disturbance range from vague possibilities to real and immediate worries. A travelling husband frequently encounters risks (health and otherwise) not common in the United States, and this may contribute to her unrest.

Some react magnificently and others, as one might expect, go to pieces.  In view of the importance of the wives in the overseas team, we would do well to devote some energy to studying them as a group— both for the benefit of recruiting and for what we might learn in general about the reaction of humans to significant changes in patterns of living.

X

# Looking Ahead

"A brave world, Sir, full of religion, knavery, and change: we shall shortly see better days."

—Aphra Behn, *The Roundheads*

The future of Colombia can be very bright. It has recently made remarkable progress in many sectors of its national life. A substantial amount of industrialization has taken place. An extremely difficult political dilemma amounting to civil war has been at least temporarily solved. Substantial financial stability has been attained. Diversification has progressed. Public transportation has been expanded and improved. Increased educational opportunities have been made available at all levels. These things, and others, have demonstrably occurred, but one must beware of over-optimism for the future. There are serious problems yet unsolved, problems so grave as to jeopardize already realized progress. Unless concrete achievement is made shortly in solving some or all of these problems, serious repercussions can be expected.

A high U.S. government official complained in a conversation that overseas economists were not doing an adequate job of selling "free enterprise" to underdeveloped countries. It was suggested that he did not know what he was talking about. I asked him about specific aspects of our "free enterprise": "Do you approve of the Sherman Antitrust Act? Do you approve of minimum wage legislation, public education, public roads, the Federal Reserve Act, the tariff, the Pure Food and Drug Act, the Taft-Hartley (or Wagner) Act, agricultural subsidies, the Post Office?" With some variation of enthusiasm, he approved most of these. "Now," I asked, "tell me more about this 'free enterprise' system that you want us to sell."

This attitude is related to Colombian problems in its clear implications to U.S. aid policy. We gringos have some strong notions about what we expect in underdeveloped countries, to be discussed briefly before turning to specific Colombian problems. Parenthetically, it is appalling how naive is the image of "free enterprise" carried overseas by some and which they feel should be somehow adapted or adopted by newly developing countries. The aforementioned gentleman clearly had the notion that somehow we should sell nineteenth century "free enterprise" to the Colombians when the majority of U.S. voters want no truck with such a system at all.

United States interest in the underdeveloped countries is for the most part a portion of our overall foreign policy and arises from threats in the cold war. We seek allies among these nations—or as second best, countries which will be "neutral" in our favor. In seeking these objectives and somehow connecting them with "free enterprise" or "capitalism" or whatever one chooses to call it, we dangerously confuse that which is essential with that which is nonessential and perhaps that which is possible with the impossible. That which is essential to us is friends, countries which can be counted upon to aid and support us and peoples who are genuiently commited to the ideals of individual freedom, self-determination, and real political independence, and those who respect the rights of others to the same freedoms. These are the real issues before the world and not whether the State is going to own all the factors of production or only a part of them or whether the State is going to utilize three-fourths of the national product or only thirty per cent of it. It is commitment to our "ideals" that is *essential,* and what is *nonessential* is the form of the economic system which our friends choose to adopt. There is little objection to the economic system of the Soviet Union; our real struggle with it is on ideological grounds concerning the freedom of men, singly and collectively, to determine their own destiny. We should stop confusing the democratic ideals that we want people to choose and support with some fuzzy notion of "capitalism" which is not nearly so important. Insisting upon devotion to "capitalism" in the underdeveloped countries may prevent or retard their development in the material sense and, more important, in the democratic sense. This is the confusion between the "possible" and "impossible."

It may seriously and conscientiously be argued that it is not possible for democratic ideals to exist or to develop in a "socialistic" economy. Just as seriously and conscientiously, it may be argued that they can. A knowledgeable socialist would argue that democratic ideals would be much more likely to flourish in a socialist environment than under nineteenth century capitalism.

Be this as it may, it is not certain that capitalism as we knew it in the early days of our development is even an available alternative to currently underdeveloped countries. In the first place, they have lived for decades and even centuries with "free enterprise" or *laissez-faire* economies, and these have failed to provide improved living standards for the great majority of the people. The cynic says that this nineteenth century capitalism has clearly kept most of the people in the nineteenth century. These countries did not experience any functional democracy with their capitalism, and in too many cases they had not even the forms of democracy.

It was asserted that many of these countries may not have the alternative of capitalism as an economic system, and this is a real possibility. Political power and economic power is typically concentrated in the hands of a very few people. Political power came to be concentrated in these hands initially because the people were poor, illiterate, conquered and because they had no heritage of education and freedom. In conformance with the previously stated objective of fostering democratic ideals in these countries, it is clear that the political power "pie" must be divided so that a much greater share goes to the masses. Concomitantly, these same poor and downtrodden must have improvement in their economic well-being which means that the economic power "pie" must be divided to give these people a relatively greater share. It may be that the wealth "pie" can be made bigger so that all will have more. In any case, the poor must have relatively more and it is doubtful that the pie can be increased in size sufficiently quickly so that the rich may retain the same absolute amount while the masses get substantially more.

This leaves us with the unhappy conclusion that the economic strength and the political power of the current elites must be shared with the masses if U.S. objectives are to be met (to say nothing of the objectives of the majority of those people directly involved). Only an extremely enlightened elite will be willing voluntarily to abdicate its economic power (wealth), and so long as it keeps its economic power, its political power is apt to remain intact.[1] And what are the prospects that *laissez-faire* capitalism will lead countries out of this? What chance does the little guy have in his life-time? How can he ever be *our* friend if we keep trying to sell him the economic system that has been instrumental in keeping him behind economic and political eight balls?

The above paints the picture in its blackest terms—perhaps. Some countries, to be sure, have more enlightened elites than others and some have more democracy than others. Where *evolution* is possible within the available time limits (and these limits are terribly short in many countries), it is preferable to *revolution* with all its excesses, wastes, and inefficiencies. Colombia is a country where evolution has a good chance, but the problems which face it are enormous and time is short.  These problems are the subject of the remainder of this chapter.

*Political.*  Colombia's political problem has many implications and facets, most of which were described or alluded to in Chapter III. Political peace and progress is clearly the most important task for the immediate future.  A respite and time to produce more fundamental solutions has been found in the expedient of the National Front.  The hold of Laureano Gomez was broken, Rojas Panilla deposed, and substantial peace and tranquility achieved.  But this is an uneasy peace. A large share of the national budget still is absorbed for national defense (i.e., internal policing).  The reins of the government are still very much in the hands of the oligarchy through the apparently paradoxical alliance of the Liberals and Conservatives.

This association has merit if only because it brought peace in ending a virtual civil war.  This peace should be providing a breathing space in which sincere, radical, and constructive reforms are undertaken to bring something of hope to the Colombian masses.  But the Liberal-Conservative coalition of the elite plus the two-thirds voting requirement in the congress has resulted in little or nothing being accomplished in the way of constructive policy.  It was often rumored that President Lleras would resign rather than serve out his full term because of his inability to get any major legislation approved.

The present government must use what little time remains to convince Colombians by action that it has the interests of all Colombians at heart.  The only two alternatives for the oligarchy are: (1) to participate as leaders in a reformation of the Colombian economic and social system, or (2) to watch the reformation from afar—Heaven (or some other theological location) or perhaps from Miami in company with their Cuban *compadres.*  The present operation is no real alternative— banding together the two major elements of the oligarchy in an effort to maintain the *status quo,* throwing only as few sops to the bulk of Colombians as absolutely necessary.[2]

As urgent as is political reform in Colombia, there are certain factors which suggest that the threat of a social revolt is less immediately severe than in some other countries.  In the first place, per capita incomes are higher than in many underdeveloped countries.  There is poverty, abject poverty, but it is not in the same class as that of India, Haiti, Bolivia, and others.  There has been some development with new employment opportunities appearing in industry, commerce, transportation.  With these new opportunities, a middle class has been developing.  The Church is probably stronger than it is in Cuba, for example, and this strength is thought to be a deterrent to revolution.[3]

Finally, there is in Colombia no convenient whipping boy on whom all troubles can be blamed and against whom popular support can rationally and irrationally be rallied. Foreign investment is not large, and it is widely diversified. With the exception of one sizable investment in oil production (Colombian Petroleum Company), foreign investment is largely in manufacturing (e.g., Phillips, Goodyear, W. R. Grace) and services (Sears, I.B.M., Pan American). These types of investments with production for the domestic market do not carry the same "exploitation" connotations as frequently do extractive industries. One would be hard pressed to demonstrate that extractive industries really take anything more out of the country than manufacturing industries,[4] but this very likely appears to be the case to the citizen of the capital-receiving country. What he thinks and how he feels are of paramount importance whatever the logic and data may indicate. Until now there has been little agitation in Colombia against foreign investors, and the pattern of this investment is such that it will be difficult to use this as a focal point of unrest as the Cubans were able to use the "sugar monopolies."[5]

Thus, Colombia's problem is first of all political. Now that relative peace has been obtained, immediate steps must be taken to convince the Colombian that there is hope for improvement in his well-being and that he can have confidence that improving his welfare is high among the objectives of the government.

As a corollary to this, it is important that the government be made more real to the average Colombian. It is now very distant; and he views it with some fear, a good deal of mistrust, and considerable indifference born in historical performance. Specifically, my suggestion involves considerable decentralization of some aspects of governmental activity even at the expense of efficiency. And there is no clear case that efficiency would be negatively affected. As it now stands, local government (the *município*) collects very little in taxes and has very little autonomy in decision making. Roads, schools, extension service, are the responsibility of some higher unit of government.[6]

The connection between government services and the taxes paid (mostly indirect in the low income levels) is not an easy one for the sophisticated to see, much less the small farmer. In addition, the principal executive officer of the *município* is appointed by the governor of the departament and his responsibility lies there, not with the people of the community. It would be very wise to seek some areas of governmental activity which can be made the sole responsibility of the *município* so that people can participate directly in the process of government and see the immediate results of their participation. This might require some technical assistance from experts in the departments or in the national government, but even if there are mistakes and the pattern is spotty, I think that this would be a most useful undertaking.

In a situation such as is found in Colombia, it is easy for the gringo to favor decentralization for the sake of decentralization because it is the system with which he is more familiar. Colombia now consists of sixteen departments and some other minor political organisms. As noted earlier, Colombia has an area equal about to the combined areas of Texas and California. If we ignore the sparsely populated plains, this leaves an area somewhere between California and Texas in size. This is much too small to divide up into thirteen or fourteen sovereign "states" in a federal system such as we have. There may be room for more autonomy in the departments, but this is not a crucial issue, nor would the benefits gained by increasing autonomy here begin to match those of increased independence in the *municípios*.

*Land Reform.* This is perhaps Colombia's most important economic problem although it has important political and sociological overtones as well. In comparison with some other countries, it is an extremely complex problem, but it has its compensations as well.

The "problem" has several components.[7] There is the typically Latin American tendency to hold land in *absentia* as a prestige asset and as a hedge against inflation rather than as an income producing asset. Thus, considerable potentially productive land is kept out of production simply because the owners neither need to use it or care to use it for income producing purposes. Alternatively, they may use it for second-choice uses, such as grazing cattle instead of cropping because this is less bother. This practice was evident in Boyacá where the flat fertile valley was being used for cattle grazing while the surrounding mountainsides were being planted to potatoes, barley, and fruit by poor farmers on a small-plot basis. The possible political ramifications of this practice are obvious.

In some areas, consolidation of holdings is more appropriate than further division. Cotton and rice have become major crops in the Plains of Tolima—both in relatively recent times—spurred partly by trade protection and partly by the inauguration of irrigation in this area. Prior to these developments, much of this land was in small subsistence farms. Both cotton and rice are crops which require large scale operations to be effective due to the machinery, dusting, etc., required. Likewise, a considerable *minifundia* problem exists in much of the coffee producing country.

Inadequate transportation facilities also distort the patterns of agricultural production. Much of mountainous Tolima, for example, is not served by road at all although the hillsides are covered with the holdings of small farmers. With the expense of shipping cash crops by burro, the only one of sufficient value per pound is coffee—and of this Colombia needs no more. Adequate transportation within the plains and from the plains to the heavily populated eastern mountains might very well transform this area from one devoted almost exclusively to extensive cattle grazing to the production of grains, fruits and vegetables. The recent completion of the road from Medellín to the coast has made enormous changes in the agricultural economy of the area adjacent to the road of the sort just suggested. It is hoped that the completion of the railroad to the Atlantic coast will have a similar effect in that area.

The final component of the land reform "problem" is the possibility that it might come about. It is no exaggeration to imagine that agricultural production might be increased by a conservative 50 per cent with only modest changes in technology if some miracle brought about an efficient use of agricultural resources. In order for this increased production not simply to glut the market, basic changes in the kinds of goods produced would be required, also a new system of agricultural marketing.

Even in 1958, fewer than 13 per cent of Colombia's imports[8] were agricultural commodities, very broadly defined. Most Colombians were not actually hungry during this year although their diet left much to be desired. Thus, one concludes that Colombia is not far from being self sufficient in its present quantity of agricultural production and that any radical change in the pattern of production which would substantially increase agricultural output would create some new problems. Some of the new productive capacity could well be absorbed in producing new goods so that the Colombian diet would include new foods and the diet would be more varied and of higher nutritional value. With the proximity of all climates—frigid to torrid, rain forest to desert—and with two oceans to draw from, Colombia could have one of the most varied diets in the world and relatively inexpensively. Providing the prospective consumers with the income to make these purchases is another problem. If the shift from agriculture to secondary and tertiary industry continues, this would absorb some of the surplus agricultural workers. Others will be involved in agricultural related industries, processing, mechanics, storage, etc. Developing new agricultural exports appears to be another real possibility. Most promising are textiles, animal products, African palm oil, cacao. At once this aspect of Colombian agriculture makes the problem more complicated and less complicated. While the political aspects of the situation are pressing, the economic realities are less urgent than if half the population was literally starving. This provides certain degrees of freedom in approaching solutions to the compound problem that would not be present if both the economic and political aspects required immediate solution.

One other feature makes the land reform program appear favorable if the political elements can bring themselves to regard it seriously. There is apparently considerable marginal land available for colonization and expansion which can be made useful and valuable with relatively little effort. Specifically, the Medillín-Coast road and the Atlantic railroad are opening up new lands. This may be of special importance in attacking the coffee problem which is discussed below.

*Coffee.* In the late 'twenties, Brazilian coffee production climbed to such proportions that its price fell in world markets far below what was acceptable to Brazilian producers. This began the famous "valorization" schemes which at times variously involved burying coffee (until someone calculated that a hole about the size of the state of Rhode Island would ultimately be needed), dumping it into the sea (but it killed too many fish), and burning it (but it doesn't burn well, and floating a loan from the principal consuming country to buy kerosene was required). Valorization was successful—to such an extent that Colombia was able to enter the coffee markets and with its mountain-grown "milds" to take a fairly large portion of the world's coffee market away from Brazil. Valorization on an international scale is now being attempted—through the Inter-American Coffee Agreement during World War II and more recently through international agreement of most of the New World producers. Basically, the effort is to raise prices by permitting only certain national quotas to be marketed. History truly repeats itself, as the African producers, more or less new in the international market, wanted no part of the agreement and are now taking an increasingly large share of the market from Latin America.

Colombia's coffee problem is essentially one of producing more coffee than it can export under its quota and than it can consume domestically at what are regarded as acceptable prices by the producers. There is nothing new in this situation to the U.S. observer as compared with our own agricultural problems of surpluses except that coffee production depends so heavily on foreign markets.

There are elements in the coffee problem which make it difficult to solve. In the first place, it is a labor intensive commodity, generally farmed in small plots (frequently the growers are owners) on hill or mountainsides. These may be quite inaccessible because the high price per unit of weight (as compared to other crops such as potatoes, corn, yucca, etc.) will permit slow and expensive transportation. Thus, solving the problem will involve (1) the displacement of considerable numbers of people from coffee growing, (2) finding a substitute cash crop in a most difficult geographic and agricultural situation for those people who cannot be moved, and (3) finding industrial opportunities or new agricultural opportunities for people who must physically leave the coffee growing areas. There is no clear or easy answer to such a problem as the history of our own struggle with agricultural surpluses attests. Again, the United States may be rich enough to afford continued subsidization of the agricultural segment of our economy, but the economy of Colombia has too many other things that must be done and that cannot otherwise be done to continue to devote excessive resources to the production of coffee—only to be stored to keep it off the market.

*Education.* There is no alternative, either, but to make immediate efforts to alleviate the problems of the lack of educational facilities. This problem has two facets, one of which can be disposed of in short order. More total resources and attention must be devoted to education. The more complicated question arises when one attempts to reach conclusions about where the greater emphasis ought to be placed.

In the long run, it is highly desirable that the level of literacy be increased, for only if this is done is there any possibility of the development of a democracy. This is an objective on which agreement can be reached. It, however, will do little to solve short run or immediate problems. One of the most pressing of these is in agriculture where the level of literacy is the lowest, conservatism as related to technical change the highest, and where conditions and hopelessness are most appalling. These people still constitute the largest proportion of Colombians and as indicated above, agriculture is Colombia's most impressive economic problem. Perhaps the greatest changes in the future and probably the most painful adjustments must come in farming. It is imperative that considerable attention be given to planning for these changes, that agricultural extension and vocational training in agriculture be undertaken seriously with the objective in mind of easing the adjustment of Colombian agricultural workers and resources to the total of Colombian development. The cooperative seems to me to hold considerable promise as a device for collective improvement by the farmers, but ignorance, individualism, and mistrust have not yet permitted the development of this form of economic organization to any substantial degree.

Education is likewise required for the developing industries—more than just vocational education although this is needed badly enough. We need to know more about the problems of industrializing an essentially rural population and the difficulties of adjusting to urban living and industrial discipline. Both sides of the labor market could benefit considerably if some means, whether through formal education or not, could be found to ease these transitions. Especially, much effort should be devoted to the development of union leadership and a better understanding of the role of unionism in an industrial economy. Employers are now prone to regard the unions as communistic *per se*, and union leadership at the second level is terribly weak, sometimes dishonest, and frequently irresponsible.

It has also been already noted that there is a severe shortage of second line executives both for government and business. Providing these people is the business of the universities. The basis for doing this is already fairly well established, but the resources devoted to the task are inadequate. Even without an increase in the resources devoted to higher education great improvement could be achieved by increasing cooperation between existing and now uneconomically competing institutions and if more appropriate pedagogical practices were adopted. Higher social values will have to be placed on certain applied fields (*e.g.*, agriculture above all) before the numbers and kinds of people needed can be attracted to these areas.

There is no clear answer to the problem of how scarce resources ought to be devoted to competing and urgent educational needs. Most of my emphasis at this point would be placed on education in agriculture, broadly defined, because of its great importance to the development of Colombia and the role which it can play in that development. An honest effort at using education, too, to ease the problems attendant on industrializing would pay large social dividends both in terms of productivity, smoother and less painful urbanization, and perhaps in reduced political friction. General education has waited for centuries, and, although I dislike seeing this neglected, it can wait a bit longer.

If emphasis is put on the two areas suggested above, many, many people will be directly affected by the educational arrangements, and most urgent developmental needs will be met first. My suggested priorities neglect training of junior executives for government and business. This portion of education in Colombia is now further advanced than the others mentioned. For the time being, I believe this can be continued adequately with a relatively smaller share of expanded education budgets.

*Planning.* The general subject of planning is related to the failure to solve the major political problem, and it is related to the failure to face realistically the land reform necessities. But it is more general than either of these. There has been a general lack of appreciation of the size of the problem of development and its nature. There is little appreciation for the necessity of approaching it in broad terms—of looking at the various existing components of the economy and studying the nature of their interrelationships. This is, of course, the first necessary step.

Beyond this, there must be thinking of the possibilities of development and what changes in these structural relationships will be necessary if development is to proceed along one of several lines. Further, what "planning" for development is taking place is being done on extremely short-run and pragmatic bases. A much longer view of the situation ought to prevail or at least be coexistent. The present operation, hardly worthy of the title "planning," has resulted in a series of opportunistic, uncoordinated policies (sometimes inconsistent) which have little relationship with any rational plan for long-run objectives.

In part, this lack of consideration of the long term and really of the basic problems of development has been due to the preoccupation of the government with other problems which it regards as more pressing —peace, integration of various segments of the population into the political and economic structure of the nation. As important as is the necessity of putting out brush fires as they develop, no really coordinated policy for development will take place so long as the government is restricted to the role of fireman. Some resources of the government must be devoted to preparing long range policies for development. These must be regarded as the most important government activity although specific proposals may not enter the political arena soon or frequently. The government must put some of its most competent people into this task, do what is necessary to keep them on the job for a considerable period of time, and keep them out of the anti-incendiary activity.

There exists now a national planning commission which consists of several "counselors," a "chief" of the department, and a staff. During the course of about a year and a half, this chief changed twice, and the counselors several times, and the staff was just being developed. Unfortunately, the function of the committee was largely as economic advisor to the president and it became much too much involved in the daily tasks of decision-making. In this role, little attention can be given to those things which ought to be its principal concern.

Establishing such a group will not be easy where the process of government is insecure and where continuity of government is doubtful. This is one of the inherent weaknesses of democracy at its best, but when the democracy is weak, this weakness of not being able to look beyond tomorrow is increased in apparently geometric proportions. Good people must be sought for this task, they must have the confidence of the major political factions, their mission must be understood, and they must be freed from the day-to-day rough and tumble of politics.

Development of a group with such characteristics will not be an easily accomplished task for a country such as Colombia. But it is something which is required. There is nothing in the history of Colombia or of most other presently underdeveloped countries to indicate that development will come about automatically. The evidence seems to be quite the reverse in most cases. Nor does it appear likely that significant development will come about as the result of a whole series of marginal steps taken on the spur of the moment to solve (or to try to solve) immediate problems. Too frequently, these marginal steps are inconsistent with each other and very probably inconsistent with any reasonable long range plan which might be developed. Government must play a crucial role in this development, but first it must decide what the nature of this development *can* be and what its role *will* be. Then, Colombia can get about the business of developing along sensible lines.

❈     ❈     ❈

Those problems discussed above are those which I regard as fundamental problems. This chapter is concluded with two areas which are important but clearly do not fall within the same category of importance: trade policy and the development of a tourist industry.

Both of these are rather jumping the gun and getting to the specifics of a "plan" before that plan is developed, but they are of importance and of interest. Furthermore, they illustrate clearly the relationship between developmental planning as I have outlined it above and the nature of present policy.

*International Trade.* Colombian trade with other nations is characterized on the export side by heavy dependence on coffee exports as we have already noted. Imports are diversified with a large percentage going to capital equipment and raw materials and intermediate products. It is not really meaningful to describe Colombia as having a dollar shortage unless this is simply understood to mean that she could use more dollars (i.e., foreign currencies) than she currently has. This latter interpretation is quite correct—as it is for most countries, and for that matter, most people. Imports are severely limited by a licensing arrangement which contributed heavily to the appreciation of the peso in 1959 and 1960.

It is the two principal features of the trade picture, heavy dependence on coffee for exchange earnings and the usefulness of additional exchange which leads me to emphasize this problem especially. Colombia is more advanced industrially than neighboring Ecuador and much more diversified and more advanced industrially than another neighbor, Venezuela. Yet in recorded trade (i.e., "legal") in 1958, less than 1 per cent of Colombian exports went to Venezuela and an infinitesimal amount to Ecuador. In part, this is the result of tradition and the historic erection of trade barriers by these two countries, but more important than that is the Colombian attitude toward these sources of foreign exchange. These markets demand products which are not traditional exports for Colombia whose trade is by far greatest with the United States. These markets will take industrial products—china, shoes, textiles, leather, appliances, tires, meat. But each time that these have become export possibilities, the Colombian government has placed export quotas on the products, the argument being that sending these goods out of the country will deplete the domestic supply and thereby raise the domestic price. This is an extremely shortsighted policy in view of the shaky nature of the coffee exports, the desirability of diversifying the export list, and the need for increasing supplies of foreign exchange. This is one case in point where day to day decisions based on immediate political expediency leads to policy inconsistent with long range *desiderata*. It clearly is in the long run interest to diversify the list of exchange earners and to continue to expand the industries which are doing apparently rather well in the domestic market.  In most of the cases noted above, it is doubtful that exporting a portion of the domestic product would lead to domestic price increases anyway; the expansion of production and marketing facilities most likely would lead to reducing prices.  It seems clear that Colombia has a chronological advantage in the development of these industries and should be exploiting it fully while the opportunities exist. Thus far, there has been little consideration of these longer run implications of export policy either in terms of specific products, and the attitude toward the idea of a common market arrangement has been equivocal.

*Tourist Industry.*  Next to nothing has been done to exploit one of Colombia's greatest natural resources—its convenience, its variety, its beauty, and its appeal for the U.S. tourist.  Perhaps Colombians and resident gringos alike will not thank me for urging the development of this industry.  Most countries hit by the tourist hordes claim not to like it, but they are grateful for the ever increasing flow of dollars. And these are available for the taking.

The principal obstacle to present tourist traffic is the lack of tour promotion either by the government or privately.  Rarely, compared to Pan Am's ubiquitous eulogization of Mexico, does one see Avianca's advertisements concerning Colombia.  Nor is the internal organization of the tourist service industry ready to accept large quantities of tourists.  Most of the facilities are adequate, and only filling in certain gaps would be required.  Fine hunting and fishing, all varieties of climate, magnificent scenery, historic sightseeing sun-swept beaches, low costs, gem mining, good hotels and food, picturesque rural life— what more could the tourist ask for?  With little effort, this would indeed become a major source of foreign exchange for emerging Colombia.

# References

## CHAPTER I

1. This translates to: Center for Studies on Economic Development. Both its English and Spanish names are too long to live with, however descriptive, and it is referred to hereafter as "CEDE", pronounced "say-day".

2. International Bank for Reconstruction and Development (Lauchlin Currie, Chief of Mission), *The Basis of a Development Program for Colombia,* Washington: 1950. United Nations, Economic Commission for Latin America, *Analysis and Projections of Economic Development: III. The Development of Colombia,* New York: 1957. Misión "Economia y Humanismo," *Estudio sobre las Condiciones de Desarrollo de Colombia,* Bogotá: Comite Nacional de Planeación, 1958. See also the more specialized but very useful, International Bank for Reconstruction and Development, *The Agricultural Development of Colombia,* Washington: 1956.

## CHAPTER II

1. This describes horizontal classification at the first level below the national government. Vertical organization is described below.

2. Departmento Administrativo Nacional de Estadistica (DANE), *Anuario General de Estadistica,* Bogotá: 1958, pp. 3-4.

3. Boyacá has not been included as one of the political units of the *llanos* in the preceding tabulations because a major portion of it lies in the mountains.

4. Still anouther route exists further north and even more direct. As late as April, 1960, however, I was advised not to try it even by jeep.

5. Politically, departments or *departamentos* correspond to states, although they have much less autonomy. They are composed of *municipios,* roughly the equivalent of counties. These are the lowest form of formal political organization and combine the functions of counties, townships and cities in U.S. organization. *Municipios* do, however, contain *veredas* (something like the township), but these are an informal arrangement.

6. DANE, *op. cit.,* pp. 19-20.

7. By May, 1961, the rate was back again to about 8; in April, 1962, it was approximately 9.

8. Manizales may be said to be the coffee capital of the world in terms of fine coffees. Colombian coffees are called "milds" in contrast to the less desired but more plentiful Brazilian coffees. Milds sell for more in the New York markets and are blended with Brazilian coffees to give "body" and "flavor." Some coffee enthusiasts wax eloquently about their drink in the literature. See, for example, Andris Uribe C. *Brown Gold,* New York: Random House, 1954, for an unintended amusing account.

9. I use the term "gringo" to apply generally to citizens of the United States, although this is not its precise meaning—if it has one—and although it has a connotation of disapprobation when used by a Colombian. It is strange that we have

no proper adjective or noun to describe U.S. origin. "American," so much used, is grossly improper as it describes anyone from the Western hemisphere. *Norteamericano,* as used by Colombians, at least narrows the field down by one continent. In Spanish, a suitable term does exist *estadounidense* (literally, "United Statesian"), but this is (1) awkward, (2) difficult for the *gringo* to pronounce, and (3) subject to the puristic objections that it is not descriptive either as there are even in Latin America (also a misnomer) such other countries as the United States of Brazil and the United States of Venezuela. For the most part, I will us the term "gringo" to indicate U.S. origin.

10. Even so, many rural communities are without "adequate medical care"—an extremely relative term in cross-cultural comparisons.

## CHAPTER III

1. Pittsburgh: University of Pittsburgh Press, 1957.

2. It was his assassination which touched off the bloody debacle in April, 1948, during the meeting of the leaders of the Western Hemisphere republics. This was, incidentally, remembered by cities about to become host to such a meeting, e.g., Quito, 1960.

3. Ernesto Camacho-Leyva, *Quick Colombian Facts,* Bogotá: Instituto Colombiana de Opinión Pública, 1957 (2nd ed.), p. 53.

4. This "boycott" was something less than voluntary. For a good description of the rough and tumble politics of this period, including assassinations, shootings during congressional debates, etc., see Fluharty, *op. cit.,* Chap. VII.

5. See Fluharty, *op. cit.,* for his analysis of this coup. pp. 118-158.

6. Camacho-Leyva, *op. cit.,* p. 41.

7. Colombian names are sometimes confusing. Generally three names are used, such as Alberto Lleras Camargo. The first is the given name, the second the family name (i.e., "last" name), and the final is the maiden family name of the mother. The structure of an unmarried woman's name is the same. When she marries, la senorita Delia (given name) Moreno (family name) Mejia (mother's maiden name) becomes la senora Delia (no change) Moreno (maiden name) de Restrepo (husband's family name). During President Lleras' visit the U.S. in April, 1960, newspapers discussed the visit of President "Camargo"

Confusing as it may be, we ethnocentric gringos should have the curtesy to find out and to use our guests' names properly.

8. New congressional elections were held in March, 1962. The presidential election follows in May.

9. "A Note on Democracy and Underdeveloped Countries," *Current Economic Comment,* August, 1955.

10. Property or educational attainment restrictions on the right to vote, as found in many parts of the world, can be considered as an attempt to limit the control of the masses in the government. More sympathetically, these can be regarded as crude devices to limit the electorate to persons competent to understand and decide issues. On this basis, discrimination as to sex makes no sense, but limitation as to age (as also a crude device to eliminate the incompetent voter) does.

11. Departmento Administrativo Nacional de Estadistica, *Anuario General de 1958,* p. 194.

12. See Chapter VI for a more detailed discussion of education.

13. Abel Naranjo Villegas, *Memoria del Ministro de Educaión al Congreso de 1959* Bogotá: Imprenta Nacional, 1959, p. 9. (Translation mine.)

14. *Ibid.*, Chap. XVIII.

15. Fluharty, *op. cit.*, pp. 316-17.

16. Let it not be thought that Colombia has any monopoly on this. With the political sophistication and high level of education in the U.S., our collective decision making leaves much to be desired in many areas.

17. This followed close on the heels of major riots in Mexico ostensibly for similar reasons.

18. This is not the place to press the merits of the argument except to note that in many cases, expanded production can lead to lower unit costs, better quality, and better merchandising.

19. This is common knowledge, and Cúcuta is one of the most bustling of little towns. All sorts of stories arise. One of the more charming involves the little peasant who approached the border with a cart of hay. His name did not appear on the "paid-off" list of custom officials, but they could find nothing amiss and so he was permitted to cross. The following day, he returned from Venezuela—cart, hay, and all. This persisted week after week to the great mystification of the customs officials. They could never find any contraband in the ever-present hay. Months later, after being relieved from his post, the customs inspector met the now prosperous *campesino* on the street and asked him to explain what he had been doing. "Oh, señor, I was contrabanding carts. I went over with a new one and came back with an old."

20. See pg. 13. As with rice, it is interesting to note that the higher priced and prestigious refined product costs more than the more nutritive, unrefined product.

21. Most of these policies were inherited by the National Front and were not of its making.

## CHAPTER IV

1. There is no detailed agreement on either point. See the standard works on the general subject of economic development: Benjamin Higgins, *Economic Development*, New York: W. W. Norton, 1959, pp. 6-9; W. Arthur Lewis, *The Theory of Economic Growth*, London: George Allen and Unwin, Ltd., 1955, p. 9; Charles P. Kindleberger, *Economic Development*, New York: McGraw-Hill Book Company, Inc., 1958, Chap. I; Gerald Meier and Robert E. Baldwin, *Economic Development*, New York: John Wiley and Sons, Inc., 1957, pp. 2-10. See also my "The Development of Low-Income Countries," *Papers*, Michigan Academy of Science, Arts, and Letters, 1952.

2. Data to and including 1953 are from CEPAL, *Analisis y Propecciones del Desarrollo Económico: III, El Desarrollo Económico de Colómbia*, New York: United Nations (1957. II. G. 3), 1957, p. 35.

The figures for 1957 and 1958 are not strictly comparable. They were computed from a Colombian categorization of imports "Importación de articulos importantes, 1957-1958," the total of which constituted 68 and 67 per cent of all imports in those years. Departamento Administrativo Nacional de Estadistica, *Anuario General de Estadistica*, 1958, Bogotá: Imprenta Nacional, 1958, pp. 629-633. There is no reason to assume, either, that goods were classified exactly the same by both agencies.

3. For 1957 and 1958, DANE, *op. cit.*, p. 629 ff. For 1946, Dirección Nacional de Estadistica, Controlaría General de la República, *Anuario Anual de Estadistica,* 1946, p. 274 ff.

4. For 1925, 1945, and 1953, CEPAL, *op. cit.*, p. 17. For 1958, Servicio Nacional de Aprendizaje, *Aspectos Quantitativos de la Población Colombiana y sus Relaciones con la Disponsibilidad de Mano de Obra,* Bogotá: June, 1959, p. 21. Data for 1958 are not necessarily comparable and are based on projections, not censuses. The reliability of both sets of data is unknown.

5. Derived from data of the Banco de la República, published in mimeograph, without title or date. Totals do not equal 100 per cent due to rounding.

6. Banco de la República, *op. cit.*, for income figures. For deflating, I used "Indice de Precios de 15 Articulos Alimenticos de Primera Necessidad en el Pais, Indice Nacional," *Revista del Banco de la República,* various numbers. "Current" pesos indicates no adjustment for price changes.

7. Comisión Economica para América Latina (Economic Commission for Latin America), abbreviated CEPAL (ECLA).

8. Derived from data from DANE and Dirección Nacional de Estadistica Controlaria de la Republica, *Anuario de Comerico Exterior,* various years, and G.P.O., *Statistical Abstract of the United States, 1959,* p. 329. The statistical methodology used leaves much to be desired, but nonetheless the proper impression is conveyed.

9. For 1957, for example, all agricultural production for the U.S. was 4.5 per cent of the national income of the U.S. G.P.O., *op. cit.*, p. 305.

## CHAPTER V

1. The best work on this subject is International Bank for Reconstruction and Development, *Agricultural Development in Colombia,* Washington: 1956.

2. Guillermo Franco C., *Mercadeo de la Papa Respecto a Bogotá,* Bogotá: Universidad de los Andes (CEDE), 1959.

3. The Commission on Higher Agricultural Education sponsored by the W. W. Kellogg Foundation, *Higher Agricultural Education in Colombia* (unpublished second draft), 1960, Statistical Appendix, Table 8.

4. See A. C. Pigou, *The Economics of Welfare,* London: Macmillan, 1932, 4th ed., p. 20.

5. *International Economic Coperation,* New York: Elsevier, 1945, p. 106. For a further elaboration of this point, see my "The Development of Low-Income Countries," *Papers of the Michigan Academy of Science, Arts and Letters,* Vol. XXXVII, 1951, pp. 283 ff.

6. It is clear that these maxima are not necessarily mutually consistent. The tenets of capitalism hold, for example, that incentives to produce are found in the possibilities of earning more—the larger the contribution to producing what society wants, the greater the reward. If this is the case in any given society, equality of income distribution by fiat would reduce production incentives and thus total income. Then, one may have to "buy" some greater equality with some production if this is desired. But it does not follow that the greater the inequality, the greater the production. In the first place income inequality does not all stem from production—some comes from speculation, graft, inheritance, etc. In the second place, we know little about how much in the way of reward

must be offered to attain given levels of productive effort. To some extent, the same is true of stability. It may be possible that greater productive progress will be made with high degrees of sectoral instability and individual insecurity than with great stability and personal security.

7. John M. Hunter and James Anthony Short Ternent, *Población, Ingresos y Requisitos de Capital, Colombia,* 1957-1975. Bogotá: Universidad de los Andes (CEDE), 1959.

8. The capital coefficient used here was 4. For greater detail, see *ibid.,* and for a general treatment, see Jan Tinbergen, *The Design of Development,* Baltimore: The Johns Hopkins University Press (IBRD), 1958.

9. For general works, see Note 1, Chapter IV. For a more unorthodox and well presented point of view, see Albert O. Hirschman, *The Strategy of Economic Development,* New Haven: Yale University Press, 1958.

10. This and other related points are treated at some length in my "Reflections on Administrative Aspects of a Technical Assistance Program," *Economic Development and Cultural Change,* July, 1959.

11. Realization of this point will result in drastic changes in U.S. foreign policy *vis à vis* such countries.

12. This problem is discussed in greater detail in my "Dilemmas of Public Control in Underdeveloped Countries," *Business Topics,* (Michigan State University), Summer, 1959.

13. In *The Voice of Latin America,* New York: Harper and Brothers, 1961, p. 157.

## CHAPTER VI

1. This section is based on a study of the teaching of economics in Colombian universities made in June, 1959. John M. Hunter and James Anthony Short Ternent, *La Enseñanza de la Economía en Colombia,* Bogotá: Centro de Estudios sobre Desarrollo Económico, Universidad de los Andes, 1959. A much shorter version was published in the *Journal of Inter-American Studies,* Spring, 1960. All comments refer to undergraduate instruction as no graduate work is offered.

2. A *facultad* most nearly resembles the "college" in U.S. university organization. It has a *decano* or dean, offers degrees, has considerable autonomy and is responsible directly to the chief administrator.

3. See my "Qué es la Economía?", *Revista del Banco de la República,* March, 1960.

4. Actually, this was further confused by two different categories of "full-time"—*"tiempo completo"* and *"dedicación exclusiva."*

5. This results in some most appalling student schedules!

6. Literally, "eye meter." Figuratively, "a guess based on observation."

7. One person, for example, was the vice president of a large corporation. When our study was made, he was teaching courses in three different universities in Bogotá during his "off duty" hours. Neither money or prestige were his prime motivations as his position provided both.

8. These comments are concerned with training the "economists" in the limited sense. They are also true of business administration objectives. The graduating Colombian probably will have much greater responsibilities than his gringo counterpart who typically leaves the campus for a corporate "training program."

9. This section is related to my "Comentarios de un Gringo sobre la Educación

Universitaria en Colombia," *Revista de la Universidad de los Andes,* March, 1960.

10. Even if we had a device to give us the "proper" amount to be spent on education, this would still leave unanswered the problem of distribution of that amount between the various possibilities within education: Higher education versus primary and secondary education; classical education versus vocational education; Shakespeare versus soil science; etc. These are important decisions to which much attention should be devoted.

11. DANE, *Anuario General de Estadistica,* 1958, pp. 193-194.

12. U.S. Government Printing Office, *Statistical Abstract of the United States,* 1960, p. 105.

13. James Anthony Short Ternent with Alfonso Vergara Samudio, *Problemas del Pequeno Agricultor en Climas Calidos del Tolima,* Bogotá: Centro de Estudios sobre Desarrollo Economico, Universidad de los Andes, 1960, Cuadro B-30.

14. There is, as a result, a good deal of fraud perpetrated by some of these institutions.


CHAPTER VII


1. This kind of religious limit to consideration of alternatives is not unique to Catholicism. The Judeo-Christian ten commandments severely limit freedom to seek solutions to problems. Eskimos are said to solve their population problems by turning the aged out to freeze or starve when their productivity declines.

2. In purely economic terms, these church buildings are usually properly regarded as a misallocation of resources. But this may not be the case when the community's present and to-be value systems are taken into account. That is, the construction of a large church in a small, rural community would produce fewer economic goods and services than, say, a community irrigation project of equal costs. But the spiritual values received from the church might be far greater than whatever economic values ensued from the irrigation project. This would cast considerable doubt on the validity of the "unverified probability" of Pigou. See page 45.

3. For various comments regarding these problems, see: Norman S. Buchanan and Howard S. Ellis, *Approaches to Economic Development,* New York: The Twentieth Century Fund, 1955, p. 80; Wendell C. Gordon, *The Economy of Latin America,* New York: Columbia University Press, 1950, p. 164. A Curtis Wilgus and Ranl d'Eca, *Outline History of Latin America,* New York: Barnes and Noble Inc., 1946, p. 141; Chester L. Hunt, "Cultural Barriers to Point Four," in Lyle W. Shannon, *Underdeveloped Areas,* New York: Harper and Brothers, 1957, p. 318; Benjamin Higgins, *Economic Development,* New York, W. W. Norton, 1959, pp. 219-224. The last reference discusses the Weber-Tawney thesis which concerns the relative merits of Protestantism and Catholicism as "culture" media for economic development.

4. For a more detailed recounting, see my "Experiences in Developing an Economic Research Center in Bogotá," *International Development Review,* June 1961.

5. To complete the census, one naturalized Colombian had such a degree and one native Colombian earned his degree in agricultural economics.

6. Respectively, William J. Lederer and Eugene Burdick, New York: W.

W. Norton and Company, Inc., 1958, and Walter Adams and John A. Garraty, East Lansing: Michigan State University Press, 1960.

## CHAPTER VIII

1. Some emerald waste and imperfect formations find a market in the Far East where their powder is thought to have aphrodisian qualities.

2. See Chapter III.

3. At least a thorough search of DANE, *Anuario de Comercio Exterior, 1958*, Bogotá: DANE, 1959, failed to turn up a classification which included emeralds.

4. Michael Weinstein, *The World of Jewel Stones*, New York: Sheridan House, 1958, pp. 65-66. Chapter four of this work concerns emeralds and is an interesting, non-technical account. Two books of an adventure-autobiographical nature provide entertainment as well as a good impression of mining activities in Colombia. See Russ Anderton, *Tic-Polonga*, New York: Doubleday, 1954 and Peter W. Rainier, *Green Fire*, New York: Random House, c. 1942.

5. Beryl is the basic component of many stones of much less value such as aquamarine, morganite, and the various brown, yellow, and pale green beryls, Weinstein, *op. cit.*, p. 62.

## CHAPTER IX

1. East Lansing: Michigan State University Press, 1960. For a more general study, see Harlan Cleveland and associates, *The Overseas Americans*, New York: McGraw-Hill Book Company, 1960.

2. *Ibid.*, p. 77. No better point of departure could be found for most of this essay!

3. ICA (International Corporation Administration of the Department of State) became AID (Agency for International Development) during the Kennedy Administration.

4. But I hasten to add a bit to the folklore on the other side of the ledger. One university-contract person insisted on cataloging Vietnamese government publications under "foreign government publications" in a *Vietnamese government library!*

5. In Saigon, for example, housing was extremely short and a nicely furnished bungalow of five rooms costs about $600 per month. The choice was clear: either furnish housing or an adequate housing allowance or do without professors.

6. We are not butter users at home; Colombian margarine is unpalatable except for cooking.

7. The justification (rationalization?) for this generally is the substantial amount of entertaining that is supposed to be required. As a doubting Thomas concerning the ability of the "cocktail" to accomplish anything, I cannot support even the basic premise of this argument.

8. See also Adams and Garraty, p. 70.

9. I do not want to overemphasize this, for I can hear the reader saying to himself, "Oh, that I had such problems to adjust to!" More folklore: At Christmastime, 1955, we entertained at dinner some sailors from a U.S. naval vessel in the harbor at Saigon. I impressed the cook with the need for something special and he proudly showed me rare beef filets that he had bought. By dinner time,

these had been turned into hamburgers.  Reason:  in looking through U.S. magazines, he had seen countless pictures of hamburgers and thought them a great delicacy for us.  What could I say?  This proved more hilarious than not, but peppermint flavored shrimp (who dampens initiative?) proved a bit of a flop. And have you ever seen an *ironed* accordion-pleat drip-dry skirt?

10. Quoted above.

11. The glamour fades rapidly as the flow increases.

12. Pp. 68-76.

13. Pp. 49, 151.

## CHAPTER X

1. A pilot study was made of personal economic power in Colombian corporations.  As "power" was measured in this study, 2.52 per cent of the persons studied had 28.44 per cent of the power; 5.47 per cent had 49.80 per cent and 15.97 per cent had 81.30 per cent of the power.  Eduardo Wiesner Duran, *Control Personal de la Economia Colombiana,* Bogotá: CEDE, Universidad de los Andes, Monografia No. 6, 1960.

2. If the reader thinks that this is an exaggerated position, he is referred to C. Wright Mills, *Listen, Yankee,* New York: McGraw-Hill Book Company, Inc., 1960. This book concerns Cuba, but there are many other "Cubas" just over the horizon.

3. It is not important in the present context whether one considers this a desirable or reprehensible attribute of the Church insofar as the long run is concerned.  The writer feels that to the extent that the Church is a strong and conservative influence, this permits *for the present* the possibility of bringing about radical social changes through evolutionary as opposed to revolutionary changes—which he regards as desirable.

4. Only if it could be shown that extractive industries earn a greater net return or that they repatriate a greater percentage of the same net return would this be true.

5. This general contention is supported by Eduardo Wiesner D., "Barreras Artificiales a la Inversión Extranjera en la Industria Nacional," *Revista del Banco de la República,* No. 387, January, 1960.

6. See Javier Alvarez C., *Finanzas Públicas Departamentales y Municipales Comparadas en Colombia, 1957,* Bogotá: CEDE, Universidad de los Andes, Monografia No. 5, 1960.

7. See, especially, IBRD, *The Agricultural Development of Colombia,* Washington, IBRD, 1956.

8. Computed from DANE, *Anuario de Comercio Exterior de 1958,* p. 8, ff.